What Others Say

Dr. John Ellas has done it! At least once a week, I receive a call from someone in a church asking about an effective tool to measure their local church. They want to know how to evaluate, plan, measure church growth and be the church God wants them to be. This book is one of a kind. Dr. Ellas has been a research consultant for churches for years. Now, this great servant has provided a tool for you to research, evaluate and plan how to be an evangelistic church. The work is solid, well researched and scholarly. But, it is so understandable the local church can use this book to get great results for the Kingdom of God.

Ray Fulenwider, *Minister, Central Church of Christ, Amarillo, Texas*

Just as computers were once available only to the biggest institutions but are now a common fixture in every home and office, so the ability to crunch church numbers accurately and helpfully has only been in the hands of a group of trained church growth analysts. Now, thanks to Ellas, every church has the ability to do some fundamental church data evaluation. *Measuring Church Growth* is concise and clear. It has a motivational context and methodological intent.

Harold Shank, *Pulpit Minister, Highland Street Church of Christ, Memphis, Tennessee*

Many church leaders know neither how nor where to begin to diagnose the health of their local church. In *Measuring Church Growth*, John Ellas places in our hands a most valuable tool for interpreting the condition of the local church. In a day of declining and plateaued churches, Ellas' pages offer major help in assisting congregations in growth renewal.

J. Wayne Kilpatrick, *Pulpit Minister, Homewood Church of Christ, Birmingham, Alabama*

Measuring Church Growth is a much needed book because it provides a forecast of the future for a congregation. It provides signs of growth or decline so that corrections can be made. I commend John Ellas and the Center for Church Growth for continuing leadership provided for the growth of the church.

Clayton Pepper, *Founder of* Church Growth Magazine

John W. Ellas is director of the Center for Church Growth in Houston, Texas, which helps churches of Christ to learn and apply effective methods for growth.

John holds the D.Min. and certification as a Church Growth Consultant from Fuller Theological Seminary, Pasadena, California; the M.S. in Education from Georgia Southern University, Statesboro, Georgia; and the M.A. in Religion from Harding Graduate School of Religion, Memphis, Tennessee. He has taught at Jacksonville State University and Texas A&M University and has served as pulpit minister for congregations in Louisiana, Georgia, and Texas. Currently, John is an adjunct instructor with Harding Graduate School of Religion and Oklahoma Christian University.

Other resources from the Center for Church Growth:

Magazine
- *Church Growth Magazine* is published quarterly, and its goal is to provide effective and practical ideas to church leaders and members.

Books
- *Church Growth Through Groups: Strategies for Varying Levels of Christian Community*. Center for Church Growth, 1990.
- *Clear Choices for Churches: Trends Among Growing and Declining Churches of Christ*. Center for Church Growth, 1994.

For information on the Center's services and these resources, contact:

Center for Church Growth
P. O. Box 691006
Houston, Texas 77269-1006
(281) 894-4391

MEASURING CHURCH GROWTH:

A Research-Based Tool for Evaluating and Planning

John W. Ellas

Center for Church Growth
P. O. Box 691006
Houston, Texas 77269-1006

First Edition, 1997

All Scripture quotations are from the Revised Standard Version of the Bible, Copyright © 1946, 1952, 1971, by the Division of Christian Education of the National Council of Churches of Christ in the USA and used by permission.

ISBN: 0-9642447-2-1
Library of Congress Catalog Card Number 97-69006

Contents

List of Figures

Acknowledgments

What do space exploration, constructing a sky-scraper, playing in the World Series, and writing a book have in common? You can't do it alone. It takes help. It's a major team effort with many people making valuable contributions. Over the past few months, while completing this book, I have become keenly aware of my dependence upon so many gracious folks for knowledge, skill, feedback, and support.

Men don't like to ask for help or ask for directions, according to one observation. Well, I don't know if that is true or not. However, I do know from experience that Christians are richly blessed because God placed us into His family and gifted everyone for the common good (1 Cor. 12:7). I did ask for help and my spirit has been deeply touched by the overflowing response and encouragement from the body of Christ.

A sincere thanks to Allen Black, Jo Bryant, Cherry (my wife), Ray Fulenwider, Kent R. Hunter, J. Wayne Kilpatrick, Mac Lynn, Judy King, Gary L. McIntosh, Clayton Pepper, Pete Petree, Harold Shank, C. Philip Slate, John N. Vaughan, Carol Warren, and Flavil R. Yeakley, Jr. This book is a much better resource because of the gracious help I received. However, I do take full responsibility for its content. My prayer is that God will use it—even with its shortcomings—to bless churches for His glory.

Introduction

Most adults moving through midlife have ben-
efitted from the incredible progress in modern med-
icine. Improvements in diagnostic knowledge and
tools for identifying an illness accurately have
enabled quick and effective treatment.

Some advances have not come soon enough.
On several occasions in the early 1980s I stood by
helplessly as my wife's health slipped perilously
close to death. For nearly a decade she wrestled
with prolonged bouts of coughing and fever. On
three occasions she required extended hospitalization.

Case after case, she was diagnosed with pneumonia
and treated with antibiotics. Unfortunately the
doctors' efforts were equivalent to using a garden

hose on a three-alarm fire. She would languish under the treatment and her recovery was long, exhausting, and at times uncertain.

Not until a skilled diagnostician discovered that she had a collagen disorder (connective tissue disorder) were doctors able to treat her condition effectively. The wrong diagnosis and antibiotic treatment were almost fatal. An accurate diagnosis and treatment with appropriate medications have allowed her to enjoy the past fifteen years with a reasonable amount of good health. I dare not imagine the consequence of having continued with inadequate diagnosis.

A Medical Model

Like individuals, churches are benefitting from advances in diagnostic tools and better information. These enable a more accurate identification of congregational conditions. And they offer preventive and curative strategies for church health.

A debt of gratitude is owed to Donald A. McGavran, who was the catalyst in developing this discipline. He served as a missionary in India from 1935 to 1955. During this time he became curious about why some churches grew while others plateaued or declined. He pioneered the application of research to churches through gathering data, graphing the data, and evaluating the findings. His foundational insights lead to the church growth movement and are found in *Understanding Church Growth*.[1]

In 1972 C. Peter Wagner and Donald McGavran taught the first church growth course for American ministers at Fuller Theological Seminary. This was the beginning of American church growth thinking that matured into a comprehensive ministry model by Pete Wagner. In *Your Church Can Grow* and *Your Church Can Be Healthy*, Wagner presents a church pathology that consists of seven vital signs of a healthy church and eight barriers to growth. For a complete description and application of his medical model to Restoration churches, see my book, *Church Growth Through Groups*.

A Diagnostic Gap

A comprehensive and accurate analysis is as important to a church's future as it is to a person's health. Whether it is an inaccurate evaluation or no evaluation at all, the consequences can be disastrous—a potential decline, or worse, a slow death of a congregation. A thorough diagnosis is not beyond a church's reach; it involves three basic steps:

1. Collect the useful data that a church produces such as membership, attendance, baptisms, etc.

2. Place the data on graphs for a visual aid to reveal insights into trends and conditions.

3. Interpret the data to evaluate whether the developments reflect healthy conditions or a concern requiring attention.

Numerous books and resources are available to guide church leaders in collecting the most useful data and graphing the information. Even a greater number of books describe the healthy characteristics of growing churches and the potential barriers that prevent growth (see the selected bibliography for sources). *On the other hand, there is a dearth of information to teach leaders how to interpret the data after it is gathered and placed in a numerical format or in a graphed form.* And only a small body of objective church research exists that serves as a basis of comparison for congregations.

The purpose of this book is to make a contribution toward filling in the diagnostic gap. It is designed to be a practical tool for measuring growth trends, to provide knowledge for interpreting the data, and to encourage leaders in growth planning. It serves as a companion resource to *Clear Choices for Churches.* Efforts have been made not to repeat the same data information. Due to the new and expanded data, some findings in *Clear Choices for Churches* are updated and related to different sized churches based on the expanded research sample.

Not everyone believes that counting and evaluating are spiritual or beneficial. Chapter 1 turns to Scripture in search of the origin of numbers, counting, and record keeping. Chapter 2 addresses the frequent criticisms and gives six God-honoring reasons for keeping accurate records of growth trends.

Chapters 3 through 6 describe the useful data categories and illustrate the value of graphing. In addition, these chapters give interpretive and predictive tools for analysis that, to my knowledge, are not available in other sources. This information, along with the research findings from a large sample of growing and declining churches, forms an invaluable leadership resource.

Chapter 7 discusses the size developments in American churches and uncovers some disturbing trends in huge congregations. And finally, Chapter 8 addresses the ultimate goal—encouraging leaders to use the analysis results for church growth planning.

Data Sources

Data for the study sample was provided by churches that scheduled services with the Center for Church Growth and from research projects by graduate students in church growth. A special thanks is expressed for their love for the body of Christ and their commitment to church research and growth.

The sample includes 112 Churches of Christ with a near equal distribution between growing and declining congregations. They are located in thirty states and represent a full range of sizes and contextual settings.

It is important to note that the large sample is not a random selection, but a convenient sample. Results from a true random sample would reflect the conditions in the entire sample population. Results from a convenient sample, on the other hand, can be generalized to churches that have similar characteristics to the sample. With this caution in mind, the data offers helpful insights for comparison purposes.

The size of the sample allows a step beyond the data presentation in *Clear Choices for Churches*. The findings are divided into four groups according to church size. This allows a congregation to compare itself to growing and declining churches in its own size range. Figure I.1 shows the breakdown according to average Sunday morning assembly attendance.

Figure I.1 Church Sizes

Size	Attendance Range
Single Staff	100 - 199
Large	200 - 399
Very Large	400 - 699
Huge	700 - 1250

Several authors such as Lyle Schaller, Carl George, and John Vaughan have given a typology for church sizes. Each provides a rationale and each system has merit. The breakdown in Figure I.1 closely relates to the growth barriers most frequently observed in church growth studies. For a church in any category to grow to the next level usually requires major changes in the congregation.

The single staff churches in the sample fell within a 100 to 199 attendance range with just a few exceptions above 199. This category excluded all multiple staff congregations. Staff is defined as part- or full-time ministers while other positions such as secretaries and custodians are considered support staff. The other three groups are multiple staff churches with different attendance ranges.

The sample for huge churches has assembly attendance averages between 700 and 1250. It is very important to note that this represents the attendance range for the "1000 Barrier." Churches that grow well beyond 1250 in attendance usually have characteristics different from those that get stuck in the 1000 Barrier range. Consequently, the data findings for huge churches do not automatically apply to much larger congregations. The 1000

Barrier is further discussed in Chapter 7.

Membership figures are less reliable than attendance counts as an indicator of church conditions. Churches of Christ are fairly consistent in defining membership, as discussed in Chapter 3. Large variations, however, exist among other traditions in the way they monitor membership.

Arlin J. Rothauge presents a way to develop a comparative base using membership figures in *Sizing Up a Congregation*. By counting only *active members*, those who "demonstrate a commitment and maintain a vitality in both their worship and work,"[2] one ends up with a figure for effective comparison with other churches. He also noticed in his study that active membership figures closely compare to the average worship assembly attendance. The research, presented in Chapter 4, supports his conclusion.

ENDNOTES

[1] Each book mentioned in this chapter is listed in the selected bibliography.

[2] Arlin J. Rothauge, *Sizing Up a Congregation*. (New York: Episcopal Church Center), p. 5.

Chapter One

Biblical Considerations

Well, it finally happened. I had successfully avoided it for nearly five decades. But time and fate were not to be denied. The day came for me to spend my first night in a hospital as a patient.

In many ways it was an unforgettable experience. I never knew there were so many ways to probe, test, and measure the health of a body. After a few days the verdict was in. Based more on the test results than on my own testimony, a decision was made to let me go home. The hospital staff received no arguments from me. I was just delighted that the pictures, graphs, and numbers meant one thing— *adiós, amigos,* I am out of here.

Origin of Numbers

No one, even in good health, can escape the reality and presence of numbers. It runs much deeper than tests results, phone numbers, or a checkbook balance. Numbers are an inseparable part of nature and therefore a part of life itself. Life begins as one cell. That one cell divides into two cells and each continues to divide. As long as we live, we depend on this numerical reality. Whether we consider the inner world or outer world, numbers are present.

From the beginning, ancient peoples were faced with reoccurring and countable celestial phenomena. Before their view were days, nights, moon phases, and on a clear evening, more than a thousand bright stars to count. Curiosity led them to discover the regularities of movement in the heavens. Ancient cultures had an almost slavish devotion to celestial study. And this fascination developed into an invaluable tool for determining planting and harvesting time, for direction and travel, and for expanding their understanding of the universe.

In every field of endeavor, ancient and modern, numbers and mathematics are required. Every bridge, building, and bungalow was first designed by the numbers. All workmen—whether carpenters, plumbers, or electricians—had to work with them to complete the job. Even the clothes you are now wearing were first designed as a two-dimensional pattern that has the correct proportion for your size.

Everywhere we turn, reality is set in two or three dimensions. The page you are reading is considered a two-dimensional picture. Visually the words have length and width, but the entire book also has depth. These three dimensions are filled with measurable lines, angles, and curves. A beautiful face or an attractive body, we are told, is really a matter of the correct numerical proportions set in three dimensions. Tasty food is made possible by the best ingredients mixed in the right proportions. The list could go on and on because numbers are woven into the fabric of life.

Based on a Christian worldview, numbers are a part of God's creation rather than an invention of man. The concept and use of numbers precedes the creation of humanity. In Genesis five days of creation are accounted for before humanity appeared on the sixth day (Gen. 1:1-31).

There are systems designed by people to name and count numbers. Numbers are ideas that cannot be seen or touched. So, man-made symbols are used to stand for numbers—called *numerical systems*. The reality of numbers, however, resides in the very fabric of creation. *This makes them a divinely created gift from God for our use* (James 1:17).

Old Testament and Numbers

Scripture reveals more than a casual attitude about the use of numbers. They are utilized in counting people in assemblies, tribes, and troops; taking large population censuses; and conducting inventory accounts of accumulated wealth. Like any other gift from God, the Bible records the beneficial use of numbers and counting, and it also records their misuse.

Census taking became an accepted part of Israel's

existence. God himself commanded the first count after the exodus from Egypt (Num. 1:1-3). It provided the organizational basis for keeping track of God's people while in the wilderness (Num. 2:32-34). And it also identified the number of men available for war. There were 603,550 men over the age of twenty who were able to bear arms (Num. 1:46).

Again, after the wilderness wandering, God commanded the second census. This count demonstrated God's truthfulness (Num. 26:1-2). All of the original faithless population perished in the wilderness, and only Joshua and Caleb survived (Num. 26:65). Israel was still strong with 601,730 men over age twenty who were able to bear arms (Num. 26:51).

In each census the Levites were counted separately. There were 22,273 who were one month and older at the first census (Num. 3:43). Other counts were made for the purpose of organizing them into different areas of priestly service. For example, when Solomon began his reign, there were 38,000 male Levites thirty years of age or older ready for service (1 Chron. 23:3).

After the Babylonian captivity, Ezra and Nehemiah record the number of returning exiles. The Israelites were called together and enrolled by genealogy. Ezra's and Nehemiah's count of the assembly was 42,360 (Ezra 2:64; Neh. 7:66).

Not every recorded census was pleasing to God. Late in King David's reign he ordered a head count of Israel. His military leader, Joab, recognized the error and tried to dissuade him—but without success. Joab's report to David is revealing. He gave the number of men making up the military strength of Judah and Israel (1 Chron. 21:1-5). God's judgment fell upon the entire nation, and David's carnal motives were the culprit.

Joshua's past military campaigns had demonstrated that Israel's strength and victories came through faith in God and not through military might or numerical superiority. Before Joshua departed, he had reminded Israel that, "One man of you puts to flight a thousand, since it is the Lord your God who fights for you, as he promised you" (Josh. 23:10).

Therefore, it was not David's act of counting that was sinful. His motives for the late census were self-serving and carnal rather than designed to honor God. Originally, when the nation was turned over to the reign of David, troops were counted as they poured into Hebron to marshal support for David and form his loyal army (1 Chron. 12:23-38). However, there was a contrasting motive for counting and reporting the numbers from this early census: "For from day to day men kept coming to David to help him, until there was a great army, like an army of God" (1 Chron. 12:22). This count was to glorify God and not for David's self-glorification.

New Testament and Numbers

The New Testament writers do not shy away from presenting numbers and giving counts. Jesus employed numbers in the course of teaching Kingdom truths, and some of them imply counting. It is axiomatic that the Master would never use an evil tool to teach a godly truth. And what is true about Jesus is also true for all inspired writers.

Numbers, counting, and record keeping have a divine origin. In teaching about fear and trust,

Jesus offers comfort in the fact that God counts. No sparrow falls without the Father's knowledge and even the hairs on a person's head are numbered (Matt. 10:29-30).

To every Christian's delight, God keeps accurate records. Paul lists several of his co-workers whose names are recorded in the book of life (Phil. 4:3). John reveals more on the subject and calls it the Lamb's book of life (Rev. 21:27). It reminds me of singing one of the old favorites, "When the Roll Is Called Up Yonder." I certainly want to be there. By that time everyone will understand the right motives and eternal value of counting and keeping good records.

Luke helps us see what stands behind numbers that makes them so important to God. He places together three of Jesus' parables that are concerned with numbers. In them Jesus asked questions of His audience. If a shepherd lost one of a hundred sheep, or a woman lost one of ten coins, wouldn't they do everything possible to recover the lost item? And when they were found, wouldn't there be rejoicing? If a father lost one of two sons and the lost one returned, wouldn't there be rejoicing (Luke 15:3-32)?

The parables reveal the value of each number because each represents a human soul—a soul once separated from God and then restored to life. To make the parables' message clear, Jesus said, "Just so, I tell you there is joy before the angels of God over one sinner who repents" (Luke 15:10).

It is very difficult at times to maintain God's view of reality. Mass media have collapsed our world into a small community and flooded us with visual images from around the world of human starvation, attempts at genocide, and a population explosion of billions. It is challenging to see beyond the vast numbers and staggering world problems to see what God sees—the value of a single human soul. Jesus' parables possess the power to restore sight to our blind eyes. Observe carefully, God has valued one person's soul more than the entire material universe (Mark 8:36-37).

Faithfulness and Numbers

Today where can you place your trust? Elected officials offer bridges to the future; citizens frequently see a tightrope walk of infidelity and insincerity. Some state legislators promise that at the end of the rainbow is lottery money for education; what really happens is the poor get soaked and educators are often left in the fog of funding lies.

Big companies are also having difficulties in dealing faithfully with employees and customers. Insurance companies offer policyholders a piece of the rock, but many customers discover a sinkhole of insurance fraud. Employees of large companies are consistently assured of job security, but many consistently receive pink slips just short of retirement time. This depressing litany could go on listing other culpable institutions. More importantly, is there faithfulness anywhere? Is there anyone we can trust?

We can lift our eyes above the human condition and have assurance there is One who is faithful: "Know therefore that the Lord your God is God, the faithful God who keeps covenant and steadfast love with those who love him and keep his commandments, to a thousand generations" (Deut. 7:9). Scripture abundantly affirms that God is faithful, and it provides evidence to support the claims.

Flowing from God's love are numerous promises to those who love Him (2 Peter 1:4). In *All the Promises of the Bible* (Zondervan, 1962), Herbert Lockyer has presented a compilation and exposition of divine promises recorded in Scripture. His research uncovered one student's count of 7,487 promises by God to man. All promises are important, but a few are paramount.

God made some promises to Abraham of such magnitude they are beyond human measurement. He promised to make Abraham's descendants into a great nation, and through Abraham's seed all the families of the earth would be blessed (Gen. 12:1-3, 22:17-18). Whatever God promises, He personally fulfills. And from Genesis 12 onward, Scriptures reveal God's great acts that demonstrate His faithfulness to those promises.

Luke records the verbal defense made by the first Christian martyr, Stephen. In his historical narrative Stephen describes several of God's mighty acts in redemptive history. He begins with the promises made to Abraham and identifies Israel as the nation of promise (Acts 7:1-60). At the end of his discourse he presents Jesus as the Righteous One or Messiah murdered by the Jews (Acts 7:51-53). Peter and Paul also identify Jesus as the seed of Abraham through whom all the nations of the earth would be blessed (Acts 3:24-26; Gal. 3:16).

Luke recognizes that he is recording redemptive history in the book of Acts and providing the evidence that God is faithful in fulfilling His promises to Abraham and to Israel.[1] Luke records the growth of the Jewish and Gentile churches. He provides ample evidence of numerical growth as the nations of the earth are being blessed with eternal salvation through Jesus Christ, the seed of Abraham:[2]

Acts 2:41   "So those who received his word were baptized, and there were added that day about three thousand souls."

Acts 2:47   "And the Lord added to their number day by day those who were being saved."

Acts 4:4   "But many of those who heard the word believed; and the number of the men came to about five thousand."

Acts 5:14   "And more than ever believers were added to the Lord, multitudes both of men and women."

Acts 6:7   "And the word of God increased; and the number of the disciples multiplied greatly in Jerusalem."

Acts 9:31   "So the church throughout all Judea and Galilee and Samaria . . . was multiplied."

Acts 9:35   "And all the residents of Lydda and Sharon saw him, and they turned to the Lord."

Acts 16:5   "So the churches were strengthened in the faith, and they increased in numbers daily."

Acts 21:20   And when they heard it, they glorified God. And they said to him, "You see, brother, how many thousands there are among the Jews of those who have believed."

Jesus was not ambiguous about His earthly mission. He said, "For the Son of man came to seek and to save the lost" (Luke 19:10; Matt. 18:11). Obviously, this is a quantifiable or measurable mission. He invested His time preparing twelve other men to help carry out the same purpose (John 20:21). Jesus very strategically passed on the mission baton, not just to the twelve, but to the entire church (Matt. 28:16-20; Acts 1:8). Luke records the church's mission results in quantified terms, recognizing that God gives the increase.

God has been faithful in keeping His promises to Abraham, but the blessing to all the nations has not ended. The mission to make disciples and to mature disciples will continue until the end of the age (Matt. 28:20). God desires that more souls receive the blessing in Christ and that the church increase in numbers (2 Peter 3:9; Acts 2:47). And this, again, is a quantifiable mission.

The motive for numbering and accurate record keeping is not self-glorification. Rather, the motive springs from a sincere desire to glorify God by doing His will. In other words, church leaders want to serve as good stewards and good shepherds of their God-given mission. If we faithfully plant and water, God is still giving the increase. Counting the harvest provides an opportunity to glorify God and proclaim His faithfulness.

ENDNOTES

[1]Jacob Jervell, in *Luke and the People of God* (Minneapolis: Augsburg, 1972), pp. 41-45, demonstrates that Luke carefully documents the large number of Jews who believed, and they constitute the true Israel. Most of the numerical growth passages are Jewish conversions. Salvation must begin with the restored Israel before it can flow to the Gentiles (Acts 15:15-17).

[2]For an excellent two-part article by John Mark Hicks on numerical growth in the theology of Acts, see *Church Growth* 11, no. 2 (1996): 8-10, and 11, no. 3 (1996): 12-13.

Chapter Two

Matters of Perspective

The odds are, if you are reading this book, you already believe there is some value in keeping records, tracking trends, and using numbers as a tool for evaluating and planning. While the purpose of this text is to encourage churches in these efforts, there are inherent dangers in working with numbers.

A few of my own church consultations have surfaced some abuse of numbers. For example, attendance figures have been inflated over a period of time to perpetuate a positive impression. And in a case or two, member involvement numbers have been padded to protect a less than stellar job performance.

While these are rare cases, there is a danger of getting pride, ambition, and even job security entangled with numbers. And this causes people to see numbers as a personal threat and a potential obstacle to the purity of the gospel rather than a useful tool to help in accomplishing a mission. It is important to remember that a person's attitude about numbers is really a matter of perspective.

Criticism as Caveats

Because of a few cases of blatant misuse of numbers, most aspects of growth analysis have fallen under harsh criticism. Criticism has value as a warning about abuses. However, it should never sidetrack the church from her mission. We will look at three frequently vaunted objections to measuring growth and offer a different perspective:

1. Scriptures never command us to count numbers and keep records.

This is true. There are no direct commands in the New Testament requiring churches to count and keep records. Neither are there any directives for congregations to develop annual budgets and to balance their checking accounts regularly. But there are some major consequences that follow the neglect of such responsibilities.

As stated earlier, numbers and record keeping have a divine origin. They are tools. When used in appropriate ways, they can serve to glorify God. On the other hand, misuses can pander to human pride and self-exaltation. Let this stand as a clear warning, not a deterrent. We have numerous Biblical examples of counting, census taking, and record keeping that magnify the Lord. The church can do the same if the motive flows from a serious commitment to obey and honor God.

2. We should focus on quality not quantity; quality is what counts.

The idea here is that spiritual growth is the most, if not the only, important dimension of growth. It is true that growing in the grace and knowledge of Jesus Christ is essential (2 Peter 3:18). And it is also true that some early church growth literature was imbalanced toward the numerical growth dimension to the point that it looked like a numbers game.

Nevertheless, this criticism is unfortunate because it sets two very important Biblical mandates at odds with one another. Recorded in Matthew 28, Jesus personally handed over our mission to make disciples (numerical growth) and to teach them to observe all that He commanded (spiritual growth). The early Christians responded to that commission. And Luke records their progress without dichotomizing these two growth dimensions. He writes, "So the churches were strengthened in the faith, and they increased in numbers daily" (Acts 16:5).

3. God did not call us to be successful; He called us to be faithful.

Every Bible student would agree that faithfulness is expected of Christians (1 Cor. 4:1-2). Faithfulness is demonstrated when an individual takes the time to build a personal relationship with God and obeys all He commands.

There are problems, however, with this criticism. In most cases "success" is never defined. It is left to our imagination to leap into worldly images of large plush facilities with multimillion-dollar budgets where the megachurches are successful and all others are failures. Based on this scenario, I do not know of one single advocate of such nonsense.

Even worse, the criticism implies there is no relationship between actions and outcomes. In this view, successful outcomes have been jettisoned due to their worldly nature, so we need concern ourselves only with faithful actions regardless of outcomes.

While God did not call us to worldly success, He did call us to a Biblical standard of success. Jesus told His disciples they would bear much fruit (John 15:8,16). In verse 16 Jesus told them they would go (faithful actions) and bear fruit (successful outcomes).

"Fruit" in the New Testament refers to both spiritual growth (Gal. 5:22-23) and numerical growth (John 4:34-36; Rom. 1:13; Phil. 1:22). God is concerned with actions *and* outcomes. He calls us to be faithful *and* successful.

This objection should surface a helpful warning. God's kingdom is built with divine power. What He asks of us to do, He empowers us to accomplish. And there is no room for egotism or boasting. Jesus made it clear when He said, "I am the vine, you are the branches. He who abides in me, and I in him, he it is that bears much fruit, for apart from me you can do nothing" (John 15:5). Therefore, churches of all sizes can be faithful and fruitful, and God alone is the judge of success.

Value of Record Keeping

In a summary fashion, I will highlight some of the practical benefits of keeping good records and evaluating church growth trends in your congregation.[1] It is time-consuming and hard work, so church leaders need to catch a vision for the purpose and value of the endeavor. With the right motives, it is a valuable tool for the leader's job.[2]

1. *Record keeping creates an environment of orderliness in what appears as a chaotic world.* In the beginning God took His creation and step by step brought order to the heavens and earth. God considered this "work," but His final evaluation declares, "It was very good" (Gen. 1:31). Thorough and well-kept church records are hard work, but they also can help bring order to the world of Christian ministry and serve as a valuable tool for the leader's task.

2. *Record keeping promotes renewal by helping churches remain focused on their God-given purpose and mission.* Redemptive history recorded in the Old Testament reveals God as a God of mission. He desires to seek and restore the lost. His mighty acts in history are culminated in sending His only Son (John 3:16). Jesus accepted the passing of the Father's torch, and His Father's mission became His mission (John 6:38). Jesus concluded His work by passing the torch to the church (Matt. 28:18-20; Acts 1:8). Record keeping is the essential first step in accepting the torch and demonstrating a seriousness about the Father's business.

3. *Record keeping serves as a reminder that God has placed eternal value on every single person.* Jesus spent His earthly ministry in close personal contact with individuals including the twelve disciples. He modeled and taught about the value of each living soul. According to Jesus, a good shepherd would risk leaving ninety-nine sheep to seek just one gone astray (Matt. 18:12-14). He revealed that in heaven there is joy when even one person repents (Luke 15:10). Accurate and thorough records serve as a reminder that each number represents a soul more valuable than the entire material universe—a soul worth a shepherd's time and care.

4. *Record keeping establishes the necessary groundwork for accurate evaluation of methods.* Jesus taught that discipleship carries a high cost, and He illustrates it with two insightful parables. A person desiring to build a tower and a king facing the prospects of war would be wise to sit down and thoroughly evaluate their condition before taking action (Luke 14:25-33). Nehemiah understood the principle of wise assessment. After returning to Jerusalem, he carefully inspected the walls by night before proceeding (Neh. 2:11-18). Past church trends and present ministry conditions are often hidden from easy view. Hidden in small and unnoticed changes are trends that can affect a church's future. When brought together, these small changes can reveal large movements. Good records provide the necessary groundwork to clear the fog and unveil the trends for accurate evaluations.

5. *Record keeping forms the knowledge base for informed planning.* From the beginning God has had a plan for humankind, and He is still working the plan (Gen. 12:1-3; Eph. 1:3-6). The church is part of and participates in God's redemptive plan. Our partnership with God and His agenda is revealed in passages like: "I planted, Apollos watered, but God gave the growth" (1 Cor. 3:6). Faithful stewardship calls for informed and intelligent planning, just as good farming calls for intelligent planting and watering. Thorough and accurate records form the knowledge base for faithful planning.

6. *Record keeping reveals concrete opportunities to give God praise and glory.* The Father is presently working in our lives and in our congregations (Phil. 2:12-13). Paul opens his letter to the Ephesian church by describing the wonderful works of God through Christ on our behalf, and the appropriate response should be, "To the praise of his glorious grace which he freely bestowed on us in the Beloved" (Eph. 1:6). Unfortunately, some members are unaware of what God is doing in their congregation when there is no recording or reporting of divine activity. On the other hand, recording, reporting, and praising God benefits everyone. One of the greatest human needs is knowing that one's life has meaning. Nothing fills that need greater than seeing ways God is working through our lives and congregations. Diligent record keeping will reveal opportunities to praise God publicly and build His people.

Measurement Categories

Before we set sail into data collecting, graphing, and analysis, we must chart our course. We do not want to lose sight of the ocean for the waves. From the earlier discussion, it is easy to assume there are only two broad categories of growth—numerical and spiritual. To the contrary, growth is a big ocean with many different seas that have numerous freshwater-like tributaries.

In the field of church growth there are four major seas or categories. And they go well beyond the growth of the local church to include a world-wide mission:[3]

1. *Bridging growth.* This is accomplished through establishing new congregations across cultural and geographic barriers. Church growth is a discipline of study with its roots in the mission field. It has always held a deep concern for the worldwide expansion of God's kingdom.[4] A vital component of accomplishing this mission is planting new churches in receptive cultures both here and abroad.

2. *Extension growth.* This happens by churches extending into another community or nearby area and planting a daughter church with a similar cultural makeup. New church plants are a proven strategy for reaching church dropouts and the unchurched. Clearly, new churches grow faster than established congregations. Numerous denominations have caught the vision and regularly start new churches as a part of their growth strategy.

3. *Expansion growth.* This is growth of the local church primarily through evangelizing and

assimilating non-Christians. Evangelism is priority one, but there are other important dimensions of expansion growth such as Bible class attendance and member transfers. All are useful categories for measuring the health and growth of a congregation.

4. ***Internal growth.*** This is typically called spiritual growth or spiritual formation. It is the most difficult type of growth to measure, but it is always included under the topic of church growth. Spiritual formation is the growth of Christians in Christ-like character, in relationship to God, and in relationship to one another.[5]

A simplified approach would be to see *internal growth* as the spiritual maturing of individual Christians, *expansion growth* as the growth of a local congregation, *extension growth* as stateside missions, and *bridging growth* as foreign missions. Other terms are used to describe growth within the local church such as numerical, spiritual, and organic.[6]

The goal of this book is to provide a useful tool for local congregations so they can measure growth trends, accurately evaluate, and effectively plan. Consequently, the following chapters address only expansion dimensions of growth. Most of the typical numerical categories are discussed such as membership figures and assembly attendance. The chapters are not designed to be comprehensive. You may have other areas of equal value to track for your congregation besides those presented here.

ENDNOTES

[1]For additional insights on the value of keeping records, see George O. Woods, "What Date Is Worth Your Memory," *Pastor's Update Cassettes,* no. 5021, vol. 47, side two.

[2]Darrell Holtz, "Numbers: The If and the How," *Christianity Today* 27, no. 10 (June 17, 1983): 65. Holtz describes the positive impact upon his congregation from proper use of numbers and record keeping.

[3]For further discussion on growth typologies, see Donald A. McGavran, *Understanding Church Growth* (Grand Rapids: Eerdmans, 1970), pp. 100-101.

[4]A concise history of the Church Growth Movement has been written by Thom S. Rainer in *The Book of Church Growth: History, Theology, and Principles* (Nashville: Broadman Press, 1993).

[5]See Margaret M. Poloma and George H. Gallup, Jr., *Varieties of Prayer: A Survey Report* (Philadelphia: Trinity Press International, 1991) for an objective study of the effects of prayer on behavior and attitudes. This is one of the best empirical research studies on factors contributing to spiritual maturity.

[6]Delos Miles offers a helpful presentation of church growth vocabulary and growth typologies in *Church Growth: A Mighty River* (Nashville: Broadman Press, 1981), pp. 50-59.

Chapter Three

Growth History Vital Signs

Scripture presents a wonderful analogy of the church. The church is like a human body with Jesus as the head and each member as a vital part of the whole. When these parts work properly, health and growth are possible.

> Rather, speaking the truth in love, we are to grow up in every way into him who is the head, into Christ, from whom the whole body, joined and knit together by every joint with which it is supplied, when each part is working properly, makes bodily growth and upbuilds itself in love.
>
> Eph. 4:15-16

This analogy holds valuable implications. For example, if a person is not feeling well, he or she can go to a doctor for an exam. A wide range of numerical values are collected such as temperature, heart rate, blood pressure, and blood test measurements. From these results alone the doctor can determine if a patient is experiencing good or poor health. In essence, a quantitative body of data makes possible a qualitative evaluation. Likewise, the church produces numerical data that gives significant insights into the health of a congregation.

Fabian Policy

For history buffs, Quintus Fabius Maximus was the Roman general who defeated Hannibal in the Second Punic War. His strategy was unorthodox. Rather than a straight-out confrontation, he took a cautious approach that ended in victory. His cautious strategy has become known as the Fabian policy. I discovered the diagnostic value of this approach the hard way. The straight-forward presentation of the data findings, especially in nongrowing churches, can cause negative membership reaction. A more tempered presentation can lead to a positive reception. To avoid my mistake, consider the following observations carefully.

Numerical analysis has limitations. It is not possible to quantify every good deed like giving a cup of cold water in the Lord's name. Members of growing as well as nongrowing churches perform innumerable good works that have eternal weight (1 Cor. 3:12-15). Before the analysis results are communicated, it is imperative that members are aware of this reality and that the data analysis is only a partial picture.

In addition to good works, churches have far more strengths than points of weakness. On a regular basis, church leaders should build congregational morale by acknowledging their strengths and good works, always giving God thanks. Positive morale building is an ongoing leadership responsibility. It is needed to counter members' tendencies to lose sight of their mission and become preoccupied with a single concern or problem, resulting in low morale.

Problems are best tackled from a position of strength and positive morale. From this vantage point, numerical analysis is not viewed as a threat but as a helpful tool. It offers insights into a slice of church life by revealing areas of ministry effectiveness and others needing improvement. The Fabian policy is one of caution, reminding us that the tools offered in this book are used to build up and never tear down.

Growth History Data

Active Resident Membership

Theology as well as some practical considerations should determine the procedure for keeping accurate records of active membership. The criteria suggested below for identifying members incorporate both approaches. Regardless of how membership is defined, leaders should use consistency from year to year.

1. *Count baptized members.* This will provide a clear picture of those who have obeyed the gospel and identified with the local church. Unbaptized adults and children are tracked in other counts.

2. *Count active members.* Each church must define "active" and be consistent from year to year. Accurate counts require updating the rolls regularly. New members' names are added and inactive members removed. The larger the church, the more frequent the updating. Carelessly leaving on the active membership roles people who have moved away or individuals who haven't attended for years only clouds a diagnostic view.

Maintaining active membership counts does not imply carelessly tossing aside and forgetting about inactive members. Churches should make every effort to restore members who have dropped out. The inactive list, however, is kept separate from the active member count.

3. *Count resident members.* Some congregations host a large number of college students and others have seasonal guests. It is helpful to keep separate counts of temporary and resident members. Both are important to track, but when lumped together, the conglomerate number can mask any trends and possible weaknesses in the resident membership.

For example, a church brimming with energetic college students can give the illusion of a vibrant, young, and growing church. From a separate look at the resident membership, leaders might discover that the membership is rapidly aging and the church is ineffective at reaching resident young adults in the community. This trend would have serious long-term consequences that might remain unaddressed because it is hidden in the numbers.

Some churches have already developed a permanent record-keeping system. Others will need to start the process. Weekly bulletins often provide valuable data. If they are not available, have several long-tenured members help with establishing estimates. Have each participant provide a response, then compare and average the results. Educated guesses are useful for a start, but make sure they are documented as estimates. With this procedure it is easiest to start with an accurate count of the present data and then work backward in time in developing estimates.

Begin now to keep permanent records. Place them in durable record books or invest in one of the growing number of computer software packages for church management.

Each data category in the growth history needs eleven entries for calculating a decadal (ten years) growth trend as shown later. It is important to know that only five years can reveal a trend. Five years of growth or decline shows an established pattern. However, ten years gives a comprehensive picture for diagnosis and prescription. A congregation needs at least three years or more of growth history data before attempting an analysis of trends.

Figure 3.1 is a simple chart that can be used for recording the number of active resident members. The membership data should be the total as of December 31 for each year.

Figure 3.1 Membership

YEARS	1987	1988	1989	1990	1991	1992	1993	1994	1995	1996	1997
MEMBER-SHIP											

Morning Assembly Attendance

All heads, large and small, are counted for worship attendance. This count usually includes those in the nursery or other support ministries as well as the assembly itself. While the active membership criteria may vary some between churches, assembly attendance is a consistent measurement for comparing churches.

The morning attendance is the most sensitive barometer of what is actually happening in the life of a congregation and should receive careful attention. Membership totals will lag behind as an indicator of problems and predicaments that develop. Attendance is much closer to an immediate indicator of conditions. Some churches find it helpful to graph assembly attendance along with contributions on a weekly basis. This offers a view of seasonal trends and establishes a baseline for year-to-year comparisons.

For the growth history data, attendance should be averaged for the fifty-two Sundays of the year.

Figure 3.2 Morning Worship Assembly Attendance

YEARS	1987	1988	1989	1990	1991	1992	1993	1994	1995	1996	1997
WORSHIP ASSEMBLY											

Other Categories

Other important areas requiring a fifty-two-week average are Bible class attendance, weekly contributions, Sunday evening attendance, and midweek activities. While the types of activities conducted on Sunday evening and midweek vary from church to church, it is valuable to track the level of participation. Another area for leaders to track is total baptisms. Later we will look deeper into these categories for evaluation purposes.

Figure 3.3 Other Categories

YEARS	1987	1988	1989	1990	1991	1992	1993	1994	1995	1996	1997
BIBLE CLASS ATTENDANCE											
SUNDAY P.M. ATTENDANCE											
MIDWEEK ATTENDANCE											
BAPTISMS											
AVG WEEKLY CONTRIBUTIONS											

Calculating Growth Rates

Two calculations are standards for measuring growth—annual growth rates (AGR) and decadal growth rates (DGR). They are described below.

Annual growth rates (AGR) show how much growth or decline took place in one year. Such rates are applied to membership, attendance, and other categories that lend themselves to yearly comparisons.

For calculating AGR, take the present membership figure and subtract the previous year's figure as shown in Figure 3.4. Then divide the results by the previous year's figure. Finally, multiply the answer by 100 to convert it to a percentage.

Figure 3.4 Calculating AGR

- Present membership   500
- Previous year's membership   - 450   (subtract)
- Results   50
- Previous year's membership   ÷ 450   (divide)
- Results   .11
- Change to percentage   x 100   (multiply)
- AGR   11%

Beginning with the present data, it is possible to calculate each year's AGR and observe the trend as shown in Figure 3.5.

Figure 3.5 Membership and AGR

YEARS	1987	1988	1989	1990	1991	1992	1993	1994	1995	1996	1997
MEMBERSHIP	380	380	390	425	400	425	360	325	390	450	500
AGR		0%	3%	9%	-6%	6%	-15%	-10%	20%	15%	11%

Decadal growth rates (DGR) show how much growth or decline took place over a ten-year period. DGR is also a standard measurement that can be calculated for any number of years more or less than ten. Also it serves as a tool for comparison between churches and different time periods. Using

Figure 3.5, notice that eleven pieces of data are used for an easy DGR calculation. It is possible to get a DGR even with missing data as long as you have 1987 and 1997 data. A calculator with special functions is required to determine the DGR with more or less than ten years. See the Appendix for the procedure. The easy calculation based on the data above is shown in Figure 3.6.

Figure 3.6 Calculating DGR

- 1997 membership   500
- 1987 membership   - 380   (subtract)
- Results   120
- 1987 membership   ÷ 380   (divide)
- Results   .315
- Change to percentage   x 100   (multiply)
- DGR   31.5%

Research and Trends

Observations in the field of church growth indicate that a typical growing congregation can comfortably register 5-9% annual growth. Most growing groups can handle this amount of increase without distressing the ministry structure. Occasionally a church will surge with 20% or 30% increase in one year. Without herculean assimilation efforts, it is difficult to sustain such growth and even possible to lose the gains in the next year. This does not mean that high annual growth rates are undesirable; rather it is valuable to recognize the average range and realize the work required to generate and sustain exciting levels of growth.

A sustained 5% AGR for ten years would produce a 64% DGR, and a 9% AGR would result in a 138%

DGR. Calculate your DGR, or if you have fewer than ten years of data, use the calculations in the Appendix to establish a projected DGR. How is your church doing in comparison to the body of research among Churches of Christ shown in Figure 3.7?

Figure 3.7 Church Size and Average DGR Trends

CHURCH SIZE

		Single Staff (100-199)	Large (200-399)	Very Large (400-699)	Huge (700-1250)
D G R	Growing	38%	49%	44%	54%
	Declining	-22%	-18%	-13%	-14%

(Source: Center for Church Growth)

The Center's findings show an average range of DGR growth from 38% to 54% and the range for DGR decline from 13% to 22%. This offers some insight for comparison purposes. Church size categories are not presented to suggest one size is better than another. Chapter 7 addresses church size trends and the issue of larger versus smaller churches. However, as more data categories are discussed, it will become clear that there are differences among church sizes. And it is valuable to compare a church's trends with other congregations of the same size range.

Chapter 4

Line Graph Analysis

"**A**ll we need to count are nickels and noses. That will get the job done. Getting into graphs and analysis is treating the church like a business. Besides, you and I know that what really matters can't be graphed and evaluated."

Occasionally this myopic attitude will surface. Regardless of the motives, this stance is dangerous because, in proverbial ostrich fashion, it ignores reality. And there is nothing particularly spiritual about avoiding a reality check. Such an attitude can compromise the church's health and development.

For example, a long list or lengthy column of numerical figures can actually obscure rather than clarify a view of the church's progress and condition. Locked away in the numbers are undiscovered developments and trends. By making the figures visual through graphs, hidden realities leap out and speak volumes about ministry efficacy. And it is spiritual to use every means available to be fruitful in our God-given mission.

Simple Line Graph

Start by constructing a line graph of morning assembly attendance, active resident membership, and Sunday school attendance as shown in Figure 4.1. Before proceeding, look at your church's raw data and review the numbers. Notice how little is revealed in the numbers alone. The next step is to take your collected data and plot the lines as shown in Figure 4.1. Also calculate your DGR for all three categories.

Your DGR results may already raise some questions. Spend some *visual observation time* with your graph. Important trends will often stand out. What developments do you see in the example? Here are some of the diagnostic questions raised by the visual trends in Figure 4.1:

1. What has caused the growth momentum from 1987 to 1994 to stop?
2. What contributed to the decline in 1992?
3. What is contributing to the present decline in all three categories?
4. Why is the gap between attendance and membership getting smaller?
5. Why is the gap between assembly attendance and Sunday school attendance increasing?

Figure 4.1 Line Graph

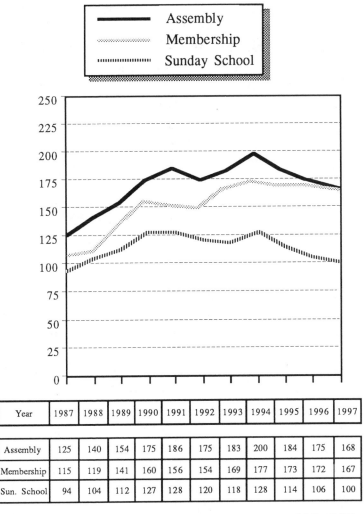

Year	1987	1988	1989	1990	1991	1992	1993	1994	1995	1996	1997
Assembly	125	140	154	175	186	175	183	200	184	175	168
Membership	115	119	141	160	156	154	169	177	173	172	167
Sun. School	94	104	112	127	128	120	118	128	114	106	100

Morning Assembly Attendance	**34%**	**DGR**
Resident Membership	**45%**	**DGR**
Sunday School Attendance	**6%**	**DGR**

Church History

From these questions it is evident that graphs reveal *what* happened; they do not tell us *why* it happened. It is essential to apply the "why" questions to the data as soon as it is collected. The farther away timewise from the data-producing events, the harder it is to discover the causes. Collecting data is an ongoing weekly and monthly activity, but graphing and evaluation should happen at least on an annual basis.

In the beginning stage, it is valuable to construct a historical background record and then keep it current along with the growth history data. On occasion, the historical background data will shed defining light on past trends. For example, if a small town loses a major industry due to a plant closing, then you may have the full explanation for a membership decline.

Here is another place for caution. Most growth or decline trends are seldom due to a single factor. There are usually several interrelated conditions contributing to a trend. Also congregations tend to look for outside factors to credit or blame for internal developments. Outside factors do play a part and on occasion they can be the defining variable, but a growing body of research indicates that most trends are more the result of ministry choices that churches make rather than outside factors such as community changes and demographics.[1]

The following questions are offered as a starting point for constructing a historical background record:

1. When was your congregation established?
2. What year did the congregation move to the present location?
3. What year was the present auditorium constructed?
4. List significant events in the church's history which may have affected the growth rate. Include events like new facilities, new evangelism program, new minister, multiple services, internal crisis, a split, planting a new church, etc.
5. List all the pulpit ministers who have served the congregation within the last ten years.
6. What is happening in the community within a three- and ten-mile radius of the church building?
7. How well do the congregation and community match?

Predictive Tools

Peering into the future has been an age-old human obsession. Whether it is ancient Greek oracles or modern-day psychics, Scripture gives ample warning about seeking the wrong sources of wisdom (Deut. 18:9-14). Jesus did indicate, however, there are common-sense signs such as the color of the sky that, when properly interpreted, can predict future weather patterns with good probability (Matt. 16:2-3).

Assembly Attendance and Membership Count

Research has identified several items that are common-sense signs with strong predictive value to growth or decline. The first predictive tool we will consider is the relationship between the morning assembly attendance and the active resident membership total. The *ideal scenario* is when the attendance figure is higher than the membership count. If this is the case, the church is most likely experiencing growth and there is a strong probability that the trend will continue. *There are some common-sense reasons for this prediction.*

First, the membership count should represent only baptized individuals. Sunday morning assembly attendance is comprised of members, members' children, and visitors. A healthy situation occurs when a church has active members and plenty of visiting guests. On any given Sunday some members are absent due to illness or travel, but that situation is offset by the number of children and visitors. Consequently, churches should monitor this relationship for diagnostic purposes. The research findings in this area for different sized churches, both growing and declining, are discussed at the end of the chapter.

Second, some congregations fail to develop adequate ministry to serve and involve its present membership. When this happens and a large number of members are not consistently attending, it is very unlikely that the church has the ministry required to attract and assimilate new members. In other words, if the present membership is not enthusiastic and involved, don't expect more to show up.

Churches can move toward or away from the ideal scenario. Figure 4.2 shows a case study of attendance and membership over a ten-year period. For the first six years this church had a growth trend with attendance averages higher than membership totals—the ideal scenario. However, you can see that the gap was slowly closing between the two. This is also true of the example in Figure 4.1. These churches had a predictive tool and an early warning sign that their growth momentum was about to end.

Figure 4.2 Attendance and Membership Growth Chart

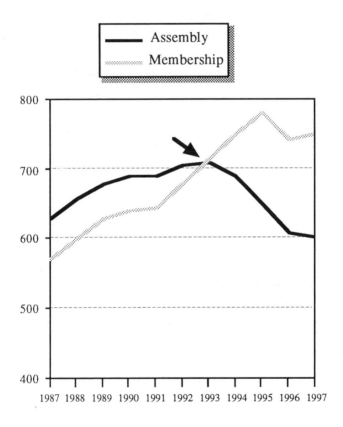

In Figure 4.2, notice in the sixth year (designated with the arrow) that membership shifted to being higher than the assembly attendance for the first time. This development in any church should raise an immediate red flag of concern for leaders. They have advance warning that the assembly attendance is about to shift from growth to decline. It is essential to start asking the diagnostic "why" questions in order to reverse the trend and move toward the ideal scenario. Leaders might discover that the church is inadequately staffed to serve the present membership size or they might discover they are short of parking and classroom space. It is important to realize that the decline trend can be reversed or even prevented if the causes are quickly identified and properly addressed.

Assembly and Sunday School Attendance

Another predictive tool is the relationship between the morning assembly attendance and Bible class attendance. *This relationship provides several predictive insights.*

First, the percentage of the assembly attendance participating in Bible classes is revealing. On average, all sizes of growing churches will have a higher percentage in Bible classes than declining churches, and the difference is significant enough to correlate with growth or decline. Growing congregations have an average 75% of the morning assembly count attending a Bible class while declining churches average only 69%. The research findings in the following section show minor variations for different sized churches.

These percentages, when tracked from year to

year, can predict growth trends and reveal ministry needs. From the line graph back in Figure 4.1 we can observe a church in transition from a growing to a declining congregation. Notice the widening gap between the assembly and Sunday school attendance.

The first tracking step is to calculate the percentage of the assembly attending Bible classes. This is accomplished by taking the average Sunday school attendance for the year, dividing it by the average assembly attendance, and converting the results to a percentage as shown below in Figure 4.3.

Figure 4.3 Calculating Sunday School Percentage

- 1987 Sunday school attendance   94
- 1987 Assembly attendance   ÷125   (divide)
- Results   .75
- Change to percentage   x100   (multiply)
            75%

In Figure 4.4 the Sunday school percentage is recorded for a ten-year period. This congregation experienced rapid assembly attendance growth from 1987 to 1991 while the Sunday school attendance also was strong. As the Sunday school attendance weakened, so did the assembly attendance growth. By the time the Sunday school attendance dropped to 64% in 1994, the assembly attendance began a clear decline trend. While this relationship would not account for all of the transition to decline, it does represent a major contributor to the decline trend.

Figure 4.4 Line Graph and Sunday School Percentage

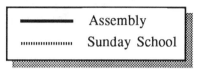

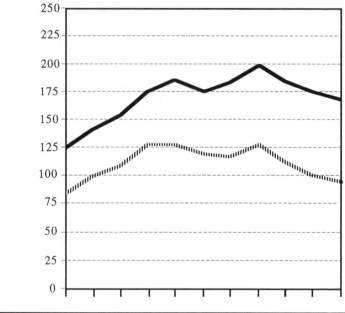

Year	1987	1988	1989	1990	1991	1992	1993	1994	1995	1996	1997
Assembly	125	140	154	175	186	175	183	200	184	175	168
Sun. School	94	104	112	127	128	120	118	128	114	106	100
Sun. School Percentage	75%	74%	73%	73%	69%	69%	64%	64%	62%	61%	59%

Some leaders have expressed surprise that five or six percentage points could really make a difference one way or the other. Well, they do! Churches cannot build a strong and stable church on assembly attendance alone. The real bonding agent for assimilating new people into a congregation is *personal friendships.* Numerous good ministry activities may attract people, but the real glue that keeps them is *relationships.* Every new member needs seven or more *friends* to feel he or she belongs. Bible classes offer the first line of offense to reach out to new people if the classes are used effectively.

This latest study confirms the research on infrastructure published in *Clear Choices for Churches.* On average, growing churches have six adult groups for every 100 members while declining churches have four groups for every 100 members. The group count includes Bible classes, ministry teams, recreational teams, small home groups, etc. In order to qualify, however, each group must have the capacity to add new members quickly and facilitate some level of relationship bonding.

Churches with more groups provide more opportunities for new people to find a place to belong. And churches that have the higher percentage of Bible class participation are also having more individuals exposed to Bible knowledge and relationship building opportunities. Consequently, churches with a strong infrastructure can endure unpleasantries in church life such as staff turnover or open conflicts. People will stay through these because of their relational bonds. On the other hand, churches with a weak infrastructure have members with looser commitments, and when the first unpleasant event happens, they head for the hills.

Figure 4.5 Sunday School Trends

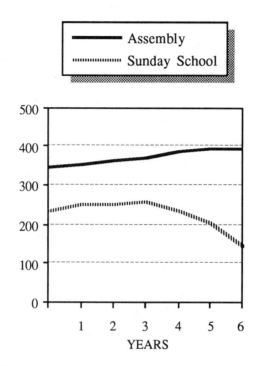

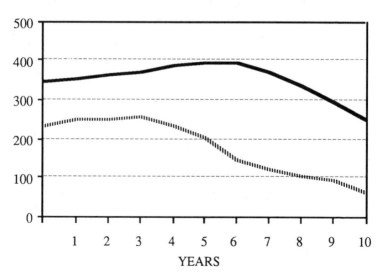

The **second** predictive insight involves the Sunday school attendance trends. For the purpose of illustration, assume we have an assembly attendance and Sunday school attendance that are basically plateaued for a period of three years as shown in the first graph in Figure 4.5. When the attendance in Bible classes begins to decline for the next three years, this is a good indicator that the assembly attendance also will soon decline as shown in the second line graph.

Even though the case study back in Figure 4.4 did not have a plateaued period, this predictive tool could have provided an early warning of future problems. Notice the attendance figures from 1991 to 1994. Even though they dipped, they reveal an upward trend. But the Sunday school attendance for the same period reveals a decline trend. Also, there was a divergence in 1993. This trend predicted a future assembly attendance decline and revealed the need for careful evaluation and ministry adjustments.

Research and Trends

This section presents the research findings and trends that surfaced in the 112-church study. The study is broken into church sizes and the significant differences between growing and declining congregations. Each figure represents the average for the category.

Figure 4.6 displays one of the strongest evaluation tools for determining ministry effectiveness. The percentage of total membership attending morning assembly reflects present conditions and is also a predictive tool as we have seen. On present conditions, it reveals the degree that the membership actively participates in the morning worship assembly. It also reflects to some degree the existing membership attitudes that impact overall ministry and it indicates the level of program effectiveness.

Figure 4.6 Percentage of Membership Attending Assembly

	Single Staff (100-199)	Large (200-399)	Very Large (400-699)	Huge (700-1250)
Growing	108%	97%	95%	96%
Declining	90%	93%	84%	88%

(Source: Center for Church Growth)

Based on the findings, a growing single staff church with 100 members would average 108 in the morning worship assembly. This means that the assembly attendance is 108% of the membership as shown in Figure 4.6. A declining single staff church with 100 members would average only 90 in the Sunday morning assembly. This means that the attendance is 90% of the membership totals.

As churches become larger, the trend is toward a lower percentage of the membership represented in the assembly attendance. Several explanations or excuses could explain the difficulty that larger churches face. Still, the ideal scenario is when the attendance average is higher than the membership. Ample case studies in each category show that such a percentage is possible and reflects the healthiest conditions. On the other hand, declining churches consistently have a smaller percentage of the membership total in assembly attendance.

Figure 4.7 Percentage of Assembly Attendance in Sunday School

	Single Staff (100-199)	Large (200-399)	Very Large (400-699)	Huge (700-1250)
Growing	76%	73%	77%	76%
Declining	69%	69%	69%	66%

(Source: Center for Church Growth)

In Figure 4.7 the percentage of the assembly attendance attending the Sunday school is given. Again it is broken down by church size and the average is given for growing and declining churches. Based on the data in both figures, growing congregations demonstrate the ability to inspire and involve a greater percentage of their members than declining churches.

ENDNOTES

[1]For a brief history of church growth research and for a related bibliography, see John W. Ellas, *Clear Choices for Churches* (Houston: Center for Church Growth, 1994), pp. 2-7.

Chapter Five

People Flow Analysis

Consider a shepherd who tends 100 sheep. He leads them into a fenced enclosure for safekeeping. A quick count of the sheep reveals that three are missing, so he energetically locates and returns them to the fold. Another, more thorough, tally shows that he is still six short of his total. Now he doubles his efforts and recovers all six. One final count uncovers the frustrating reality that twelve more sheep have disappeared. By this time he recognizes the problem—and it is not his inability to count accurately. From a perimeter fence check, he discovers that the back gate is wide open.

This story reflects real church conditions and offers insights for leaders. Most congregations have back doors that are wide open. Each year they receive new members (front door gains) and other members leave (back door losses). Unfortunately, the membership losses are equal to and often greater than the gains because the back door problem goes undiscovered and unaddressed. The best way to address the problem begins with an accurate people flow analysis. This involves tracking the numbers and sources of membership gains and losses on a regular basis.

Annual Membership Gains and Losses

Annual membership gains and losses vary little between different church sizes. However, membership trends are significantly different for growing and declining churches. Figure 5.1 shows the average gains and losses for growing churches (Group A) compared to the results for declining churches (Group B). The findings closely complement the research presented in *Clear Choices for Churches.*

Group A had annual membership gains of 18% compared to only 10% for Group B. This means that a growing church of 200 members would receive 36 new members or 18% of its membership total. A declining church of 200 would receive only 20 new members. Growing churches receive more new members through the front door, but they also lose more members out the back door. Group A had annual membership losses of 13% compared to 11% for Group B. If growing churches reduced their losses to 11%, they would experience even greater overall growth.

Figure 5.1 Average Annual Membership Gains and Losses (A)

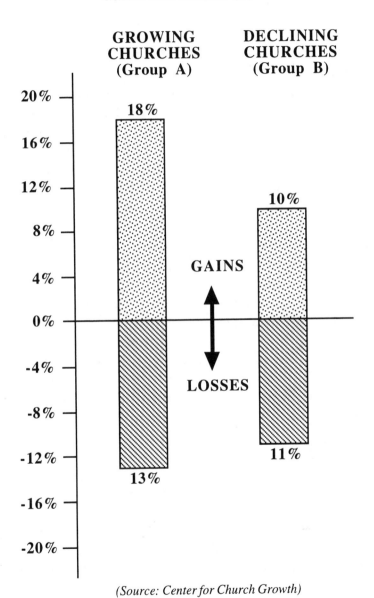

(Source: Center for Church Growth)

Leadership that considers only net gains as reflected in a line graph would miss important trends. For example, the AGR for Group A is 5% and -1% for Group B. Annual growth rates are important, but alone they leave a fog around the front door and back door issues.

People flow analysis, on the other hand, reveals that gains and losses are two different aspects of growth. What affects one does not always affect the other. Churches should see them as two different areas requiring different ministry strategies. For example, the efforts needed to attract a new member may not be sufficient to assimilate and keep that person.

It also shows leaders how many new members are required each year just to maintain the congregational size. For example, if a church of 500 members is having 13% annual membership losses, then it needs 65 new members a year just to sustain its size. And it would need more than 65 to experience growth. For this church to match the growing model, it would need an 18% membership gain (90 new members a year or an average of about two new members each week).

Collect the Data

Chapter 3 provided the basic criteria for counting active resident members. This section will go a step further and offer criteria for measuring the sources of membership gains and losses. New members enter the congregation in three ways, and a church can also lose members in three ways. Figure 5.2 is a helpful format for compiling the people flow data.

Figure 5.2 People Flow Data

GAINS	88	89	90	91	92	93	94	95	96	97
Conversions	8	10	13	4	2	7	7	6	12	15
Transfers In	25	34	35	7	7	20	23	19	29	34
Biological Growth	3	4	5	1	1	3	3	3	5	4
Totals	36	48	53	12	10	30	33	28	46	53

LOSSES	88	89	90	91	92	93	94	95	96	97
Deaths	2	4	5	1	1	3	3	2	3	3
Transfers Out	16	30	35	6	5	14	16	14	25	30
Dropouts	8	12	10	3	4	11	8	9	12	14
Totals	26	46	50	10	10	28	27	25	40	47

Membership increases through three types of growth:

1. **Biological growth** comes from the baptism of members' children. These figures are kept separate from conversion baptisms because each category reflects a very different and unique aspect of ministry. For example, Christians have no guarantee that their children will embrace the Christian faith. But, the majority of children do experience a conversion if their parents are active and the church offers quality children's and youth activities.

2. **Transfer growth** results when a church receives members from another congregation. Additional insights are available by distinguishing between new resident transfers and in-town transfers. Regardless of the reason, transfer growth is a normal and expected condition of our mobile society. The evidence is very clear. Churches with high quality and relevant ministry will receive the majority of transfers—new resident and in-town.

3. **Conversion growth** is produced when those outside the church hear the Good News, come to faith in Christ, and put Him on in baptism (Gal. 3:27). The Lord adds these to His church, resulting in Kingdom expansion (Acts 2:47). As described in Chapter 3, you want a separate count of baptisms that contribute to resident membership. Lumping together categories like college student baptisms and prison ministry baptisms results in a figure that masks the trends and perhaps even weaknesses in the resident member ministry.

The next three categories describe the sources of back door losses:

1. **Deaths** are a heart-breaking reality of a fallen world. Churches lose in membership due to the

biological death of its members. However, these are blessed when they die in the Lord (Rev. 14:13). And the church should take comfort in fulfilling its ministry of keeping people reconciled to God.

2. **Transfers (out)** contribute to membership losses for churches. People change churches for a variety of reasons. Some communities are affected by higher-than-average rates of mobility. For example, towns with large college or military populations tend to have a higher-than-average level of turnover. And transfers are a normal and expected part of a mobile society. On the other hand, some losses are due to the conditions of internal ministry. These losses offer valuable insight for ministry evaluation. It is valuable to track transfers who remain in town separately from those who move out of town.

3. **Dropouts** result when members stop participating in church assemblies and activities. Tracking these requires churches to follow up on members even if they have moved to another city. If they do not transfer to another congregation, they are counted as a dropout. Scripture reveals that some people will return to the world (Matt. 13:20-21). High dropout rates like high transfer rates, however, may signal that it is time for careful evaluation. In addition to ministries to prevent dropouts, churches need efforts to restore those who have fallen away. This group would represent an additional category of gains.

Graph the Data

Place your church's data in a graph format as shown in Figure 5.3. The people flow chart reveals the membership trends from year to year. All the columns above the midline represent the number of new members received through the front door for that year, and the columns below the midline represent the number of members lost out the back door for each year.

The dark columns indicate either biological growth (gains) or biological death (losses). Striped columns represent members who have transferred in (gains) or transferred out (losses). And the dotted columns show conversion growth (gains) or members who have become inactive (losses).

Graphing the data and making a visual analysis have the potential to uncover growth barriers that often go unnoticed in raw data. For example, is your church experiencing serious fluctuations in annual gains and losses? Figure 5.3 shows the graphed data from a church experiencing a serious drop in gains for 1991 and 1992. When trends such as these develop, leaders should immediately ask the diagnostic "why" questions in order to discover and address the problems.

Also, is your congregation experiencing a persistent problem observed in most Churches of Christ? From the case example in Figure 5.3, compare the number of new members coming in the front door with the number of members going out the back door for the same year. For the past decade, I have seen a consistent pattern for all sized churches. If they gain a little, they lose a little; or if they gain a lot, they lose a lot. Like the shepherd in the opening story, leaders who carefully study their membership trends might discover that the back door is wide open.

Figure 5.3 People Flow Analysis

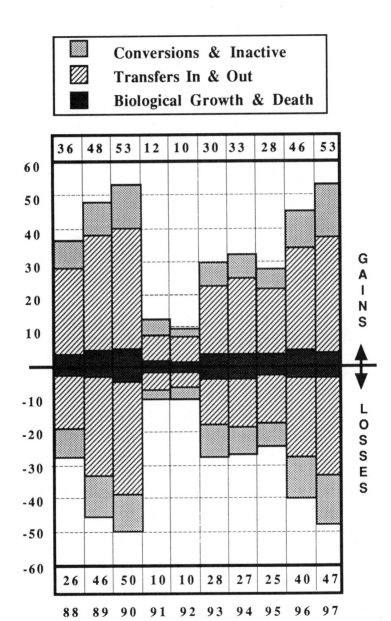

Average the Data

In order to compare your church's data with the Center's research findings in Figure 5.4, you must decide whether to use a five-year or a ten-year average. If your people flow data is mostly even and you have ten years of data, that is a good starting place. Use a ten-year average. If you have data that radically fluctuates as shown in Figure 5.3, it is best to use two separate averages, one for the first five years and another for the second five years. Remember, five years is an adequate time span to establish a trend.

Next, average the data in each of the six growth/loss categories. Another step is required to convert these figures into a membership percentage. For practice, take the transfer growth data in Figure 5.2 and get an average by adding the numbers and dividing by ten. The result should be 23.3. To convert this to a percentage of the membership, you need to know the average membership count for the ten-year period. The data comes from a church that grew from 150 to 250 members and averaged 200 in membership for the ten-year period. Divide 23.3 by 200 and multiply by 100 to convert to a percentage. Their transfer growth averaged 11.6%. These steps must be applied to each category and the results used to construct your graph. Now compare your results to Figure 5.4.

Research and Trends

As mentioned earlier, overall gains and losses vary little among different sized churches. When the data is subdivided into categories, however, huge

Figure 5.4 Average Annual Membership
Gains and Losses (B)

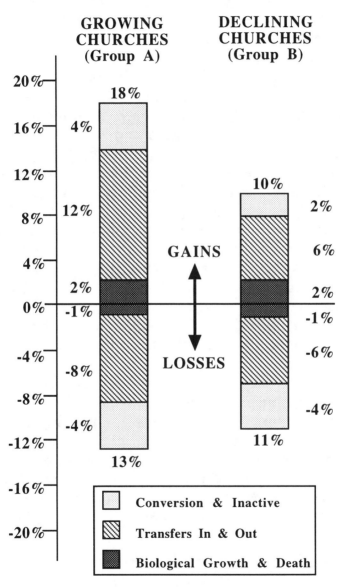

(Source: Center for Church Growth)

churches (700-1250) display a major deviation in the area of conversion growth. This will be discussed in Chapter 7. For now, Figure 5.4 shows the average for all sized churches. The significant difference is between growing and declining congregations rather than between churches based on size alone.

Based on the findings, transfer growth clearly comprises the largest portion of membership gains. Any church that does not apply intentional and effective strategies to attract and assimilate new members will sooner or later pay a very high price.

Growing congregations benefit from their efforts to evangelize and attract transfer growth. Both categories have overlapping ministry fundamentals. The same warm and friendly atmosphere required for evangelism is also a basic for attracting transfers. The end result is that growing churches double the gains over declining churches in both categories.

In other areas as biological growth, deaths, and dropout rates, there is little variation among church sizes and growth trends. On the other hand, growing churches do lose more members through transfers. Here is an important question to consider: Is that an unavoidable part of a growth scenario? From my observations of growing congregations, there is plenty of room for them to improve their assimilation ministry. The transfer losses on average could be cut to 6% rather than 8%, giving an overall annual growth rate of 7% instead of 5%.

Predictive Tools

Annual growth rates placed on a bar graph offer a powerful visual tool for predicting future trends and evaluating present ministry. Any data that is subject to an AGR calculation will lend itself to bar graphing. Useful categories to graph are found in the people flow analysis, and several other areas were introduced in earlier chapters. Some of the more helpful categories for analysis include:

- New membership gains
- Net membership gains
- Transfer growth
- Conversion growth
- Assembly attendance increases
- Bible class attendance increases
- Bible class attendance percentages

Uncover Hidden Conditions

Line graphs are a valuable tool, but they tell only a partial story. Using line graphs is like examining an arm or leg and noticing that it is undergoing atrophy (wasting away) or hypertrophy (increasing in size). Regardless of which situation appears, the observer cannot be certain about the degree of the condition. Looking at a bar graph of annual growth rates offers more of an x-ray view of the limb's condition. Issues are surfaced that remain out of sight in a line graph.

Chapter 3 described the procedures for calculating an AGR. Figure 5.5 offers a comparison of a line graph and a bar graph of the same data. From an inspection of the line graph alone, everything looks great. The church continues to register growth every year. However, hidden from easy view is a serious problem. The bar graph exposes a rapidly declining growth rate. Whenever the AGR drops from one year to the next, it is a strong predictor that the decline will continue unless properly addressed. This congregation is facing the real possibility of an attendance plateau or even a decline. This condition is mostly hidden in the line graph but made obvious in the bar graph.

AGR Lesson

Not every church follows the pattern in Figure 5.5, but this is a frequent occurrence for congregations and it offers a valuable lesson. A church cannot repeat the same level of ministry efforts from year to year and expect to keep growing. It takes greater efforts to sustain a group of 300 in average attendance than required for a group of 200. If the size increases each year and the ministry efforts remain the same, the growth rate will drop. This will continue until the church plateaus or begins to decline so that the efforts match the size.

This important lesson teaches us that, as the church grows, leaders should increase the ministry parameters. As a group expands in numbers, they must also expand their facility capacity, raise more finances, increase the staffing, and add new groups to assimilate the growth. Unfortunately, too many churches do not take advantage of these diagnostic tools. For some, it requires a crisis like a budget crunch or a decline trend before action is taken. Leaders should learn proactive strategies and stay ahead of the curve.

Figure 5.5 Line and Bar Graph
Comparison

YEARS	1992	1993	1994	1995	1996	1997
WORSHIP ATTENDANCE	175	215	249	278	300	318
AGR		23%	16%	12%	8%	6%

WORSHIP ATTENDANCE
Line Graph

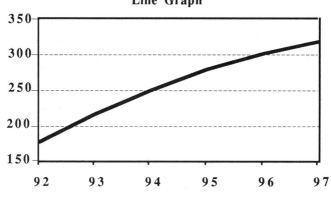

AGR
Bar Graph

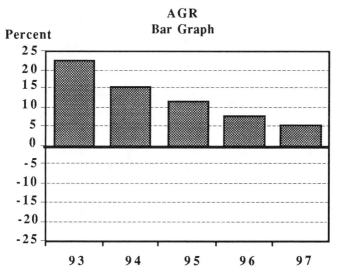

Figure 5.6 AGR Trends

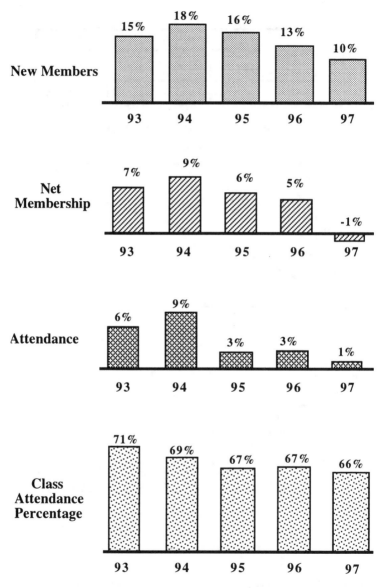

(Source: Center for Church Growth)

The final example (Figure 5.6) shows the AGR trends for a large, growing congregation. Use your insights gleaned so far and evaluate the church's condition. What do all four bar graphs have in common? What do they say about future growth? How does each category for 1997 data compare to growing or declining churches? Would this church be wise to act now or wait to see if the trends improve?

The four graphs reveal that this congregation, while registering growth, is about to plateau and possibly enter a decline phase. Each year shows a drop in the amount of growth, which indicates an inadequate ministry condition for assimilating more people. In 1994 their percentage of new members (18%) compares to the growing church model. By 1997 they have dropped to a level (10%) which matches the decline model. In fact, they actually lost in net membership in 1997 for the first time. All of the data suggests that major ministry adjustments are needed to build a growth momentum and avoid a decline trend.

Chapter Six

Church and Ministry Analysis

Scripture offers extraordinary leadership wisdom through parables describing ordinary activities like fishing, shepherding, and farming. From my modest gardening experience, I have gained a greater appreciation for lessons found in the agricultural comparisons.

For example, the knowledge that farmers have acquired about the soil holds insights for church ministry. Here are a few things farmers have learned about their land that are also true for church and ministry:

- Both are in a state of change.
- Each area has measurable characteristics that influence its productivity.
- Regular testing and evaluation are needed.
- The best methods are essential for preparing both for maximum fruitfulness.

Shouldn't church leaders have the same measure of wisdom and operate as wisely as farmers? I hope the answer is obvious. The following research findings, like the resources from agricultural science, are useful tools for ministry measurement and evaluation. If used, they can contribute to greater knowledge and productivity in the Kingdom.

Church Demographics

Soil productivity is directly affected by the balance of its organic makeup. Not enough nitrogen or phosphorus in the soil can cause a poor crop yield. Likewise, the growth potential of a church is influenced by the age distribution of its members and their children. People mix provides the context and atmosphere that promote or restrict growth.

Minor differences in age distribution exist among church sizes, but major demographic differences surfaced between growing and declining churches. Figure 6.1 shows the breakdown by age of members and children for growing and declining congregations. The findings are similar to those presented in *Clear Choices for Churches*. The latest data does, however, reveal a slight age shift that reflects the aging of the American population.

Figure 6.1 Comparison of Age Distribution in Growing and Declining Congregations

Age	Growing	Declining
Preteens	22%	17%
Teens	11%	11%
20 - 29	14%	11%
30 - 39	17%	14%
40 - 49	13%	13%
50 - 64	12%	16%
65 up	11%	18%

Age	Growing	Declining
Preteens, Teens }	33%	28%
20 - 29, 30 - 39 }	31%	25%
40 - 49, 50 - 64, 65 up }	36%	47%

(Source: Center for Church Growth)

Another way of viewing the differences in growing and declining churches is by grouping the ages into generational categories. Growing churches still show a balance between young people (0-19), young adults (20-39), and mature adults (40 up). Declining churches have a clear imbalance in ages.

When it comes to demographics, the litmus test for measuring church growth potential is the percentage of young adults in the 20-29 age range. Having this age group in the congregation speaks volumes about the attitudes and ministry efforts of a church. Other vital categories are ages 30-39 and preteens. To attract and keep the full range of adults requires a church to shift away from a self-centered preoccupation and toward developing effective ministries for young adults and their children.

When comparing your church's age distribution with the Center's findings, it is important to recognize that your community demographics for a ten-mile radius around the facility will have an influence on the church's age distribution. (For an excellent article on how to acquire demographic data on your community, see the April 1995 issue of the *Christian Chronicle*, p. 13.) Regardless of your community's makeup, growing churches usually have a higher percentage of members in the 20-29, 30-39, and preteen categories than in the community. They also tend to have a lower percentage in all of the mature adult categories. Figure 6.2 shows an example of a congregation which, at first glance, appears to have an age imbalance. But a comparison with the community demographics reveals a healthy condition where the church has a higher percentage than the community in the vital categories. There is good news, however, for the imbalanced churches. Some congregations have demonstrated the ability to regain an age balance. After discovering and owning the problem, intentional ministry strategies have enabled them to attract young adults and become a growing church.

Another demographic category that holds measurement and predictive value is *never-married singles*. A major quality displayed by growing churches is their willingness to serve *diversity*. They attract more young adults, both married and single. These

Figure 6.2 Church and Community Comparison

	Church	Community
Preteens	16% +1%	15%
Teens	13%	13%
20 - 29	12% +2%	10%
30 - 39	12% +1%	11%
40 - 49	16%	17%
50 - 64	15%	15%
65 up	16%	19%

(Source: Center for Church Growth)

two categories are like a barometer that measures congregational warmth, openness, and ministry efforts. Having a good percentage of young married and singles suggests a high probability for continued growth.

Figure 6.3 shows the different percentages of never-married singles for churches in each size range. In every case, growing congregations have a higher percentage of never-married singles than declining congregations. Another observable trend is that larger churches attract a higher percentage of singles than smaller ones do. Their size is an advantage which allows them to host a larger number of singles who in turn attract more.

The American population is shifting to a higher percentage of young single adults. Most communities already have an abundance of residents in this category. By the turn of the century, single adults (all categories) will make up 50% of the adult population. What future consequences are in store for churches if this segment remains unreached?

Figure 6.3 Percentage of Never-Married Singles

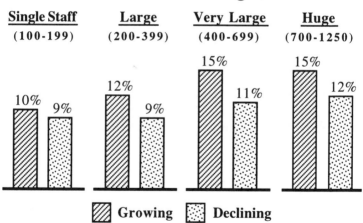

(Source: Center for Church Growth)

Budget and Giving

Herb Miller has written an exceptional book titled *Money Isn't / Is Everything* (Nashville: Discipleship

Resources, 1994). He makes a cogent point that Jesus frequently addressed money matters because how a Christian uses possessions is a spiritual matter that affects the person's relationship with God. Sixty-two percent of Jesus' parables refer to money and possessions. While the Bible includes 500 verses on prayer, it has more than 2,000 verses relating to money. From a review of the research on membership giving patterns and budget spending, some churches may discover the need to teach on a regular basis the biblical principles of stewardship suggested by Miller.

Per Capita Giving

The Center for Church Growth conducts an annual study of per capita giving patterns. A large number of churches spread across the U. S. provide us with their weekly attendance and contribution figures. Per capita giving results are obtained by dividing the average weekly contribution by the average morning assembly attendance. If a church had an average weekly contribution of $1,500 in 1995 and they averaged 100 in weekly attendance the same year, then their 1995 per capita giving was $15.

In *Separating Fact from Fiction* (Searcy, AR: Harding University, p. 24), Flavil Yeakley reported that in the late 1980s the average weekly contribution was $15 per member, and now it is closer to $20 due to inflation. The Center's study revealed a similar finding. For the 1996 study, the highest per capita giving in our sample was $33.66, the lowest was $9.43, and the median was $18.75. The Center used assembly attendance figures while Flavil used membership, but active resident membership totals closely match attendance figures as demonstrated in Chapter 4.

Figure 6.4 shows the median per capita giving for the past five years of Center data. Giving increases from 1992 to 1996 compare closely with the 4% average inflation rate for those years. As Flavil noted, giving in Churches of Christ is higher than in most religious groups in America, but giving trends remain flat when factoring in inflation. You can use these figures in the future for comparison purposes by adjusting the 1996 figure by the inflation rate, or contact the Center for the latest per capita giving results.

Figure 6.4 Median Per Capita Giving

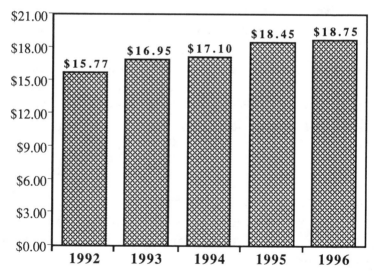

(Source: Center for Church Growth)

How is your congregation doing in this area? Several factors can affect per capita giving and should receive consideration when comparing membership giving patterns. Some communities have a higher income level than others. Large urban areas offer higher paying employment than most smaller towns and rural communities. Another consideration is the church's age makeup. Declining churches show a higher per capita giving than growing churches. Growing congregations have more financially struggling young adults and they also have more children. The number of children alone increases the assembly attendance count, resulting in a lower per capita giving figure.

So far, we have looked at per capita giving, which is one side of the giving coin. Now we need to examine the other side—weekly contributions.

Contribution Percentage

How much should a member contribute? Is tithing a goal, just a starting place, or is it just an Old Testament teaching for the Jews? Christians hold a wide range of views on this topic. Here is another equally important question that might raise less debate: When was the last time we grew in the grace of giving?

Findings presented in Figure 6.5 suggest there is a lot of room for growth in Christian giving. In the Center's study, church members were asked, "What percentage of your total family incomes does your family regularly contribute?" Those responding to the survey question represent the most active membership. If less active members had been available for input, the results would have reflected a higher percentage of members in the low giving ranges. With 57% of the active members giving 9% or less of family income, the findings suggest a serious need for regular stewardship training.

Figure 6.5 Contribution Percentage

Contribution	% Member Response	
1. Less than 2%	8%	⎫
2. 2% - 5%	20%	⎬ 57%
3. 6% - 9%	29%	⎭
4. 10% - 15%	37%	
5. Over 15%	5%	

(Source: Center for Church Growth)

These findings indicate that leaders should broaden their view of the available financial resources beyond the weekly contribution and annual budget. Churches have significantly increased their resources through strategies such as having an annual stewardship emphasis, using special contributions, and conducting capital funding drives for large expenditures. There is, however, one essential element for motivating members in stewardship. Beyond lessons on giving, members need to feel they are sacrificing for a God-sized purpose. Nothing motivates more than serving a church that can project a compelling vision for the future.

Church Budget

Scores of books and articles are available on giving and stewardship. On the contrary, it is almost impossible to find written materials suggesting criteria for evaluating how budgets are allocated. Since budgets are determined by church members, it seems reasonable that stewardship principles should apply to determining budget expenditures as well as to Christian giving. In some ways, what is true for a member is also true for a congregation; how a church spends its finances reflects its priorities and values.

Church budgets vary little among different sized congregations. Figure 6.6 shows the breakdown of a budget into eight categories and the percentage distribution for each category. A brief description is given of each category to enable accuracy in comparing the data with other churches:

Salaries include pay and benefits for all ministers, secretaries, custodians, etc.

Facilities designate the expenses for operating and maintaining the church property.

Debt retirement represents the money paid on church loans.

Education includes resources and supplies for all ages, but it does not include any salaries.

Evangelism is a difficult category, but we tried to limit it to expenses for specific evangelistic activities, training, and resources.

Missions encompasses both home and foreign mission support.

Benevolence for the most part was support distributed locally.

Other includes a wide range of expenses for ministries and activities that vary considerably from church to church.

A few exceptions to the percentages surfaced between churches. Huge growing congregations consistently have larger-than-average debt retirements. Growing attendance and additional new members motivated them to invest in facility expansion projects that created debt averaging 27% of the budget.

Figure 6.6 Church Budget

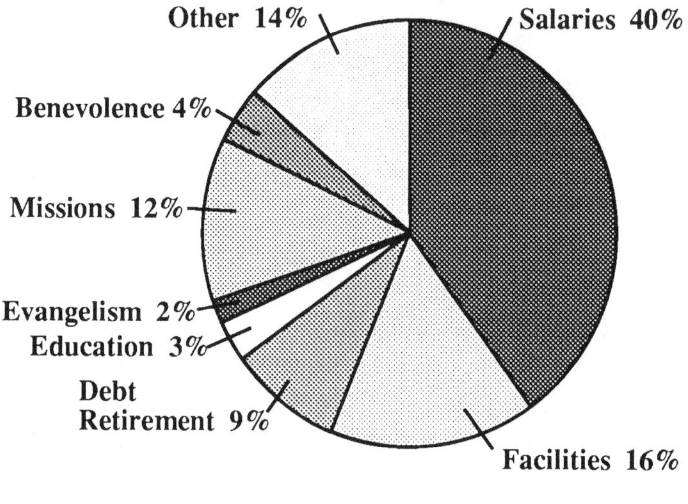

(Source: Center for Church Growth)

This is an area needing leadership caution. Wise counselors have suggested that debt retirement should be kept within a 20-25% range or lower. Growth requires investing first and foremost in ministry and staffing. If at all possible, use capital funding efforts to keep debt low and money available for ministry.

Another small exception: as churches become larger they have a slightly smaller percentage of the budget allocated for salaries. The average for a single staff church is 44%, and it drops to 36% for huge churches. This data needs some qualification and explanation.

Staffing and salaries is one area that few church members understand accurately. After twelve years and hundreds of congregational visits, I cannot recall a single church with an overstaffing problem. Instead, 95% of the churches were understaffed— some of them grossly understaffed—and still members complained about too many staff and paying too much for staffing. In these situations, leaders cannot expect more than one out of four members to recognize the understaffing problem.

The sample for this study is also a group of understaffed churches. The average of 40% for salaries should be seen as the low end of the scale. For research analysis on proper staffing for growth, review Chapter 3 in *Clear Choices for Churches*.

The final two budget categories to receive brief treatment are evangelism and missions. If a church expects its members to give graciously, shouldn't the congregation set a good example of giving at least 12% to missions? I know of no better way to demonstrate a commitment to the Great Commission than by investing in missions and local evangelism.

It is not one or the other. Investing large sums in missions does not excuse a church from local evangelism responsibilities. Numerous congregations are trying to do just that. (A more detailed treatment of evangelism is given in Chapter 7.) The 2% investment in local evangelism stands as a witness against our priorities and values. How would the Lord evaluate your church's investment in reaching lost souls?

Chapter Seven

Size Trends and Large Churches

Shopping malls, grocery stores, and universities are highly visible examples of a present cultural trend—businesses and institutions are getting larger. Churches are no exception to this phenomenon. The average congregation has tripled in size since the turn of the century.[1] People, it seems, are attracted to larger establishments for a variety of reasons like atmosphere, quality, choices, and convenience.

Other aspects of our society are getting larger and the bigger size presents more problems than benefits. The federal government, the national debt, telemarketing, pollution, and urban traffic are just a few examples. So, not all growth and bigness are beneficial. Residential communities and even some states have decided to discourage further expansion and growth. They recognize that size brings with it some unwanted problems. Our concern, however, is how the size trend is affecting congregations. *When it comes to churches, is larger better?*

Size Trends

Actually there are four distinct developments within the size trend. *First,* as already mentioned, the average size of congregations is getting larger. *Second,* by the 1970s we moved into a megachurch age. Numerous churches are becoming like giant redwoods standing among a forest of pine trees. These supersize churches average 2,000 or more in assembly attendance. *Third,* a large and increasing percentage of people are attending a smaller percentage of churches. In other words, on any given weekend, you will find the majority of churchgoers in a small number of large churches. And *fourth,* the number of congregations per 1,000 population is only half the number we had at the beginning of the century.[2]

Figure 7.1 shows the growth of congregational size for three different traditions.[3] The average increase for the combined group is 148% over an eight-decade period. This trend has had some impact on Churches of Christ. From 1980 to 1990, for example, there was a 16% increase in the number of congregations over 450 in assembly attendance and a 52% increase in churches reaching 1,000 in attendance.[4]

Figure 7.1 Average Congregational Size[3]

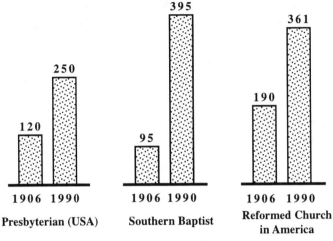

Presbyterian (USA)   Southern Baptist   Reformed Church in America

(Source: Lyle Schaller)

Figure 7.2 Megachurch Trends[5]

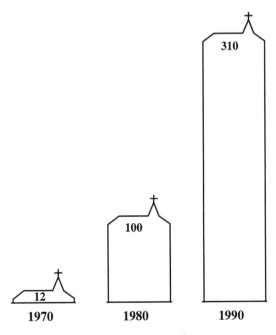

(Source: John N. Vaughan)

John N. Vaughan has made an invaluable contribution through his study and publications on the megachurch phenomenon. Based on his research, Figure 7.2 demonstrates the rapid increase in the number of megachurches.[5] In the 1970s there were about a dozen congregations with assembly attendance over 2,000. By 1980 the number jumped to 100, and by 1990 it surged to over 300. According to Vaughan's analysis, beginning in 1990, a new church reaches the 2,000 attendance mark for the first time every two weeks. This means that there are 25 new megachurches every year.[6]

Churches of Christ, for the most part, have been unable to take advantage of the megachurch development. However, the other trends are having an impact. Fifty-one percent of Protestant churchgoers attend in only 13% of the churches.[7] Likewise, 48% of the attendance in Churches of Christ is found in only 15% of the churches.[8] What is contributing to these developments? And, more importantly, is this trend healthy?

Contributing Developments

Several factors, some obvious and others not so obvious, have created an advantage for larger churches. While most of the developments are interrelated, the factors are listed separately.

1. Automobiles and highways have contributed to a mobile society. People no longer walk to church. They can drive to a church of their choice. And they are very willing to drive twenty minutes or more, passing up dozens of churches, to reach their preference.

2. America is a consumer-oriented society. Consumerism inculcates the expectation of more and better services from government, schools, businesses—and churches. It has provided people with choices, and we have come to expect choices.

3. Young adults are the most mobile age group. Also, they are the most likely source for a church to increase its membership. If they are Christians, they become church shoppers. If they are unchurched, they represent the most receptive group for evangelistic outreach.

4. Large churches usually can afford the staffing for quality preaching, teaching, and leadership.

5. Large churches have the resources in people and finances to offer a wide range of ministries such as youth programs, children's activities, multiple worship services, etc.

Consequently, an increasing number of adults are choosing to attend the larger churches. They are attracted by the array of ministries and the relational opportunities that size affords. At this point, these observations are offered as a description of the developments and not an evaluation of the trends.

Reality Check

For the past fifteen years I have spoken openly and consistently as a proponent for large churches. They are certainly here and likely to stay. At the end of the chapter we will consider some of the advantages offered by a large congregation. But for now, the Center's research findings have surfaced several disturbing trends that need consideration.

Figure 7.3 Baptisms and Church Size

Total Baptisms per 100 Members

Single Staff (100-199)	Large (200-399)	Very Large (400-699)	Huge (700-1250)

7.1   7.0   5.2   4.6   4.9

4.0   3.7   3.2

◩ Growing   ▨ Declining

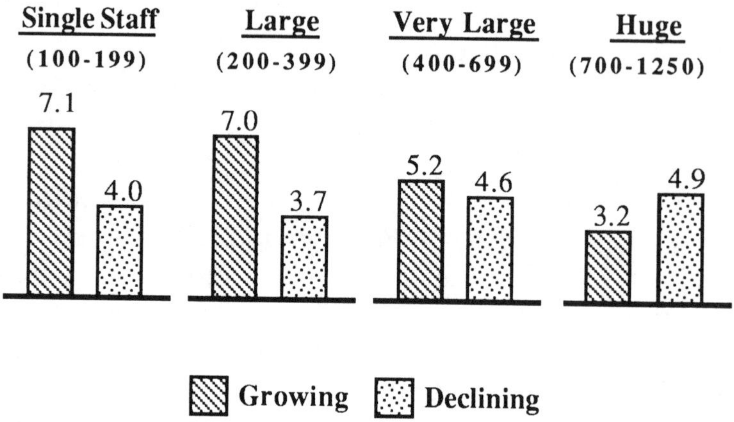

Conversion Baptisms per 100 Members

Single Staff (100-199)	Large (200-399)	Very Large (400-699)	Huge (700-1250)

5.2   4.9   4.0   3.0   2.0

2.5   1.9   1.5

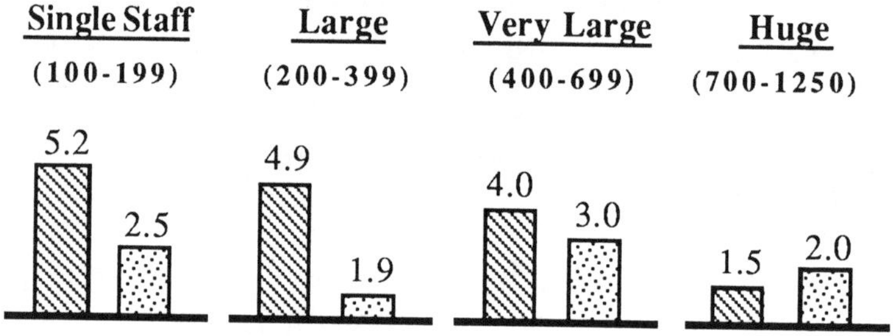

(Source: Center for Church Growth)

From Figure 7.3 at least two trends are observable. First, as Churches of Christ get larger, they decline in their evangelistic effectiveness. Second, in every size group except *one*, growing churches baptize more people than declining churches. Huge growing churches demonstrated the most unsettling trend. They actually baptize fewer converts than their declining counterparts. This represents a major divergence in the research findings for growing and declining churches and raises a host of issues that cry out for clarification and discernment.

I had heard about this trend. I had even read about it. But not until I saw it for myself did it become a sobering concern. Carl George, a leading church consultant, had observed the same trend among other traditions. He states, "Why do some churches grow even without being strongly evangelistic? The most common explanation, which fits many of the large metropolitan-area churches, is that some develop a gravitational pull on the unhappy, the disillusioned, and the underutilized from other churches."[9] Carl offers a full treatment on what he calls the "feeder and receptor patterns" of growth.

Based on the Center's findings, Churches of Christ under 700 in attendance are doing almost all of the Kingdom building work of evangelism. Even four conversion baptisms per 100 members observed in the very large sized churches is still a significant evangelistic contribution.

George Barna conducted a large scale study of evangelistic churches in America; many were huge in size and some were megachurches. Still, he found that 20% or more of their growth came from conversions.[10] Referring back to Figure 5.4 in Chapter 5, growing congregations averaged 18% annual growth and 4% was from conversions. That means that conversion growth accounts for 22% of the annual increase for the majority of growing Churches of Christ.

The only *growing* category that failed to make a significant evangelistic contribution is huge growing congregations. And adding insult to injury, declining churches baptized more than growing churches. From the pool of evangelistic research, there are few viable reasons for any sized church to average fewer than four conversions per 100 members. So, why are some churches struggling with their Great Commission mandate?

Before addressing the question, there are several other concerns that surfaced in the huge growing church data that diverge from the norms in the research. Another big surprise is that huge growing churches are not attracting a significant percentage of the 20-29 age group. This has important evaluation potential for the leadership. Figure 7.4 reveals the divergence.

Figure 7.4 Comparison of Age Distribution in Growing Churches by Size

Age	Single Staff (100-199)	Large (200-399)	Very Large (400-699)	Huge (700-1250)
20 - 29	15%	14%	15%	11%
30 - 39	17%	16%	18%	20%

(Source: Center for Church Growth)

By comparing the average age distribution in Figure 6.1 from Chapter 6 with this trend, one can see that huge growing churches are the only category unable to attract a greater percentage of the 20-29 age range than their declining counterparts. Young adults in their twenties are not attracted as much by the quality of preaching and excellence in the worship assemblies as those in their thirties. Huge growing churches usually have quality assemblies, and it is reflected in the data—20% in the 30-39 age range. However, adults in the 20-29 age range are reached through a broad range of need-meeting ministries complemented with a warm, outgoing, and accepting atmosphere. It appears that huge churches are having problems providing the level and structure of ministry needed to reach these young adults.

Finally, huge growing churches have about the same staffing ratios and infrastructure (adult groups per 100 members) as declining churches. Frequently, the supersize congregations become islands of membership anonymity and inactivity. Based on the research findings in *Clear Choices for Churches*, low staffing ratios, weak infrastructure, a low percentage of young adults in their twenties, evangelism effectiveness, and church decline are all interrelated. The big question is: How long can huge growing churches continue to increase with their present ministry efforts?

One very important caveat is needed at this point. The Center's findings are based on a particular sample and may not represent every huge Church of Christ. You may find some outstanding exceptions to our sample results. Also, as was stated in the Introduction, findings from huge churches

(700-1250) are not necessarily applicable to other large church categories such as the megachurches. Any conclusions about churches larger than our sample would require additional research.

Most, if not all of the huge growing churches in our sample will plateau in the near future unless they make some major changes. They are facing a formidable obstacle referred to as the "1000 Barrier." This barrier is not a physical obstacle, but an organizational one that affects churches with attendance ranges from 800-1200, and in some cases even higher. Few churches get beyond this ceiling because it requires several major changes that either staff, elders, or members are unwilling to make. A full treatment of this growth barrier is available elsewhere.[11]

In addition, some characteristics and attitudes are common to all sizes of growing churches, including megachurches. These are factors that must prevail even when the number of members already appears large and unmanageable.

Characteristics of Growing Churches

A comprehensive list of growth characteristics is beyond the purpose here. There are, however, a few key factors that enable congregations to move through the different size barriers and potentially become megachurches. If congregations will address these issues, they can grow regardless of their size.

1. Maximum facility use. Winston Churchill is credited with saying, "We form our buildings and then our buildings form us." Churches can become prisoners of their facilities and their comfortable pattern of activities. Frequently, congregations will allow the building space to determine the size and number of ministry offerings. A church can grow in size only if it is willing to make space for additional members.

Barrier-breaking churches creatively use their facilities to allow more people to worship and participate. Their vision is beyond a single Sunday morning assembly and Bible class period. Multiple worship services are the norm, and there is little hesitation to expand the number to three or more morning assemblies.

Leaders must monitor three areas carefully: parking, classroom space, and auditorium seating. If any one of them becomes crowded, all growth is blocked. For example, a church cannot seat any more people than it can park in a comfortable walking distance from the facilities. Creative multiple facility use requires options that ensure ample space in all three areas at every time period.

2. *Managed membership care.* I was conducting a church growth seminar and talking about the deeply relational nature of Christianity when an elder shared a fascinating story. His congregation was working hard to have an effective greeter program. On a Sunday morning, a first-time visitor entered the foyer and was welcomed by an enthusiastic greeter. The member said, "We are so very glad to have you, and we hope you find this a friendly church." To the member's surprise, the guest responded, "I am not looking for a friendly church; I am looking for a friend."

Here is a simple but profound reality. People want and need meaningful relationships that nurture the human spirit. Too many churches just don't get it. Meaningful relationships do not happen because a few classes are tossed out on Sunday morning or a couple of small groups are formed. It requires a major investment of time by qualified staff to train, organize, manage, and expand the church's care-giving system.[12]

Huge and other sized churches will plateau if they cannot expand the size and quality of managed membership care. John N. Vaughan offers this final warning, "Churches that generate their worship attendance growth through continued creation of new multiple worship services, without also creating additional small groups (i.e., Sunday school classes, and/or home cell groups), are in danger of building the empty cathedrals of the next generation."[13]

*3. **Membership involvement.*** Contrary to the small church mentality, the preacher and elders cannot provide all of the primary shepherding care for every member. This issue is interrelated with managed member care. Members must be available to one another in Christian community and ministry.

A major responsibility for staff is training and equipping members to lead relational and task-oriented ministries. As a church grows beyond 200 in attendance, its growth potential is in proportion to the level and quality of member involvement.

Staff effectiveness is partially measured by how many ministry leaders can be trained and sustained. While ministers should model ministry, their major responsibility should be the equipping of members for ministry (Eph. 4:11-12). And this requires ministry knowledge and leadership skills.

*4. **Mission driven.*** Barrier-breaking churches consistently display a high commitment to local evangelism and world missions. Based on Vaughan's study, this is also true for megachurches.[14] A growing number of research projects and case studies overwhelmingly identify the evangelism priority as a key growth variable even though our latest findings show a divergent picture with huge churches.

One thing is certain: The world's largest churches did not grow by transfers. The largest, the Yoido Full Gospel Church in Seoul, Korea, grew from five members to more than 600,000 by evangelizing a non-Christian population. Neither have the American megachurches focused on reaching transfers at the expense of evangelistic outreach. For example, the Saddleback Valley Community Church in Orange County, California, is a well known and studied megachurch with 10,000 in attendance. Rick Warren, the founding minister, writes, "Some large churches have grown at the expense of smaller churches, but that certainly is not true in Saddleback's case. The Saddleback statistic I'm most pleased about is the fact that 80 percent of our members found Christ and were baptized at Saddleback."[15]

George Barna and Thom Rainer, a professor at Southern Seminary, have entered the evangelistic research arena with C. Kirk Hadaway. Hadaway's social science research was the first to uncover the powerful relationship between evangelism and church growth.[16] Barna and Rainer have published their research findings on the characteristics of effective evangelistic churches.[17] We now have the insights for producing mission-driven churches. And we know what it takes to transition huge nonevangelistic congregations to being outreach oriented. George Barna offers three brief summary points that describe his findings:

1. The driving force behind an evangelistic ministry was the intense desire of the senior minister to emphasize evangelism.
2. Churches are marked by a philosophy of ministry in which evangelism is the centerpiece.
3. The staff and congregation "own" the mission or vision for ministry, which is largely focused upon local outreach.[18]

Regardless of the church size, nothing is more significant for breaking growth barriers than an active commitment to the Great Commission. It obviously must begin with the pulpit minister who most frequently has the members' ears. Over time, whatever passion the preacher has will become a congregational passion. Unfortunately, some ministers do not have a passion for lost souls. Thom Rainer tells a wonderful story of a minister's pilgrimage from wrestling with the authority of Scripture, to regaining an evangelical view, and the final struggle and steps to gain a Christ-like passion for lost souls. If you are not there, I highly recommend that you read about the real possibilities.[19]

Finally, evangelistic churches put their money where their mission is. Barna found that churches were investing 10-20% of the budget for local evangelism.[20] This is a major commitment compared to the average of 2% found in our study. Budgets do reflect a church's values and priorities.

Strengths of Large Churches

Earlier I raised the question, "Is the trend toward larger churches a healthy development?" Like so many complex questions, the answer is predictable: It all depends. All church sizes have strengths and weaknesses.

One thing is certain: We need all sizes of churches. When it comes to congregations, one size does not fit all. Plenty of people have no desire to be a part of a big church. And there are others who could not be happy in a small congregation.

Regardless of the size, the healthiest conditions are found in growing churches. We need big ones, small ones, and new ones. As mentioned earlier, America has fewer churches per 1,000 population than at the turn of the century. We seriously need newly planted churches in the growing urban and suburban areas of this country.[21] We also need some supersize and growing megachurches because they have some advantages over other sizes:

1. They have the finances and resources to provide specialized ministries that smaller churches cannot afford.

2. They are capable of hosting more diversity among the membership. Size allows them the ability to attract a large enough number in different ages and backgrounds to form active ministries such as singles, seniors, young adults, etc.

3. Very large energetic congregations have the potential to impact their communities. Their size gives them spiritual and, in some cases, political influence for good.

These are just a few examples of their strengths. They also have weaknesses. Members can easily evade service and involvement amidst the crowd, and leaders can easily forget their God-given mission while trying to work with so many members. Our largest churches must remember that other churches view them as a role model. They go to them, they look, and they listen. What are they learning?

ENDNOTES

[1] Lyle Schaller, "What Happened?" *Net Results* 16, no. 9 (September, 1995): 6-7.

[2] Ibid.

[3] Lyle Schaller, "3 Migrations," *Net Results* 12, no. 7 (July, 1991): 4-5.

[4] This data comes from comparing two sources by Mac Lynn, *Where the Saints Meet* (Austin, TX: Firm Foundation, 1982) and *Churches of Christ in the United States* (Nashville: Gospel Advocate, 1991).

[5] This data comes from two sources by John N. Vaughan, *Megachurches and American Cities* (Grand Rapids: Baker Books, 1993), p. 117, and *The Large Church* (Grand Rapids: Baker Books, 1985), p. 11. These resources will be republished by the author in 1998, Church Growth Today, P. O. Box 47, Bolivar, MO 65613.

[6] John N. Vaughan, "The Next Decade: U.S. Church Growth Trends," *Church Growth Today* 5, no. 4, 1990, p. 3.

[7] Lyle Schaller, *Looking in the Mirror* (Nashville: Abingdon, 1984), pp. 14-37.

[8] The percentages are drawn from the data in Mac Lynn's work, *Churches of Christ in the United States*.

[9] Carl George, *Prepare Your Church for the Future* (Tarrytown, NY: Revell, 1991), p. 31.

[10] George Barna, *Evangelism That Works* (Ventura, CA: Regal, 1995), p. 170.

[11] Carl George, *How to Break Growth Barriers* (Grand Rapids: Baker Books, 1993).

[12] For a more detailed treatment of this subject, see *Clear Choices for Churches* (Houston, TX: Center for Church Growth, 1994), pp. 80-87.

[13] Vaughan, *Megachurches and American Cities*, p. 58.

[14] Ibid., p. 88.

[15] Rick Warren, *The Purpose Driven Church* (Grand Rapids: Zondervan, 1995), p. 50.

[16] Kirk Hadaway, *Growing Off the Plateau* (Nashville: Sunday School Board of the Southern Baptist Convention, 1989), and *Church Growth Principles* (Nashville: Broadman, 1991).

[17] Thom Rainer, *Effective Evangelistic Churches* (Nashville: Broadman, 1996).

[18] Barna, *Evangelism That Works*, pp. 89-92.

[19] Rainer, *Effective Evangelistic Churches*, pp. 199-121.

[20] Barna, *Evangelism That Works*, p. 97.

[21] Flavil Yeakley, Jr., "The Need for Establishing New Churches," *Church Growth Magazine* 12, no. 3 (Third Quarter 1997), pp. 2-3.

Chapter Eight

Planning for Growth

The purpose of this book is to provide the tools for ministry evaluation and encourage growth planning. Previous chapters have shown how and what data to collect, illustrated how to graph the numbers, provided interpretive tools for evaluating the results, and revealed research on other churches for comparison purposes. If you have followed the suggestions in these chapters, the next logical step is to utilize the results for planning.

If failing to plan is planning to fail, then the outcome has an identifiable face. It is called "institutionalism." As a consultant with churches, I have looked into its face many times and have seen the frustration, disappointment, and low membership morale that it produces. For nonplanning churches, it is just a matter of time.

Institutionalism sets in when churches lose a clear awareness of their God-given purpose and they do not see a compelling vision for their future. Churches have numerous means to accomplish their purpose such as assemblies, Bible classes, youth activities, etc. These are not the purpose or mission of the church, but the means to accomplish the purpose. Churches become trapped in repeating routine activities over and over as if they were the church's purpose. They never evaluate, change, or even improve their ministries. In fact, the defense of institutionalized methods becomes more important than accomplishing the God-given mission.

Working through the process of collecting, graphing, and evaluating trends in church data is a prerequisite for planning. It can also help a church recover its mission. While evaluating the data, important questions should surface:

1. Why does the church exist?
2. What should ministries accomplish?
3. What does the Scripture say about the church's mission?

No year should go by in any church without teaching on the purpose or mission of the church. Based on Nehemiah's experience of rebuilding the walls of Jerusalem, Rick Warren believes that the church's purpose should be restated and clarified monthly.

Although the wall took only fifty-two days to complete, the people became discouraged at the halfway point: just twenty-six days into the project! Nehemiah had to renew their vision. From this story we get what I call the "Nehemiah Principle": *Vision and purpose must be restated every twenty-six days to keep the church moving in the right direction.*[1]

A renewed awareness of mission based on Scripture can serve as a catalyst for leaders to dream new possibilities even for old churches. This leads to new vision, new hope, new energy, and new planning.

Steps in Planning

The steps given below are presented as an introduction to planning and not as a comprehensive guide. Some churches have already developed their own method of planning while others may need to do some thorough homework on the planning process. It is well worth the time investment. Research supports the reality that planning significantly raises the probability of church growth and nonplanning reduces the chances for growth.[2]

At this point, I am assuming that the motivation for planning is flowing out of a renewed understanding of the church's mission and a vision for future possibilities. And finally, it is important to understand that not all of the steps are sequential; some are interrelated with others.

1. Spiritual environment. Prayer and seeking God's will should pervade every phase of the planning process. Planning is a means for the body of Christ to discern God's will for the church. Jesus said, "I am the vine, you are the branches. He who abides in me, and I in him, he it is that bears much fruit, for apart from me you can do nothing" (John 15:5). Whatever is true for one member is also true for the whole body of Christ. Church efforts apart from God are fruitless, but with Him great things are accomplished.

Chapters 1 and 2 covered several Biblical issues in this area. God is not opposed to planning. The book of Proverbs has wise counsel: "Commit your work to the Lord, and your plans will be established" (Prov. 16:3). Planning is a normal part of dealing with life, and God is able to work through our efforts: "A man's mind plans his way, but the Lord directs his steps" (Prov. 16:9).

2. *Face the facts.* For more than a decade I have shared with churches, in a public forum, their strengths and their major weaknesses. When it is done honestly, tactfully, and constructively, I have found that members appreciate knowing the truth. However, I cannot overemphasize the importance of applying the Fabian policy described in Chapter 3.

Churches should develop a tradition of presenting an annual state-of-the-congregation address. A Sunday morning sermon format works well. It is a time to review the past year's progress and help members see God's work in and through the congregation. The primary emphasis is identifying accomplishments so that God is glorified and praised. Also it is an opportunity to reveal weaknesses requiring further planning. The whole constructive enterprise is a mission- and vision-driven process.

*3. **Set goals.*** After evaluating the facts, it is time to set goals. Goals are specific accomplishments that can help a church move toward its growth vision. Based on the earlier chapters, here are a few examples that an evaluation might suggest:

- Within one year the church's assembly attendance will equal 100% of the active resident membership total.
- By the end of next year 80% of the assembly attendance will attend the Bible class program.
- The church's infrastructure will have seven adult groups for every 100 active resident members by the end of next year.
- Within two years the church will have a demographic makeup of 14% or more young adults in the 20-29 age range.
- By next year the church will average seven conversion baptisms for every 100 active adult members.

C. Peter Wagner, in *Strategies for Church Growth,* offers five criteria for setting good goals:[3]

1. *Goals should be relevant.* They must address the real problems facing a particular church. Consequently, a thorough evaluation of the church and community should precede goal setting.

2. *Goals must be measurable.* Every goal must be specific enough for measurement and have a time frame for completion.

3. *Goals should be significant.* They must be big enough that they require trust in God for their accomplishment.

4. *Goals must be manageable.* While they should be big, they should not be ridiculous. Good

goals are inspiring and not discouraging.

5. *Goals are personal.* The congregation and the leadership must have ownership of the goals.

Goal setting is often misunderstood and feared. Some leaders see goal setting as a sure way to set a church up for failure. It is better to see goals as statements of faith. After prayer and reflection, goals represent what we believe God wants to accomplish through us. After the time frame is past, measure the progress made toward the goals. Regardless of what percentage of each goal is accomplished, measure the progress and give God the glory.

Goal setting makes a major contribution to keeping a church future-oriented. It demonstrates a serious commitment to the mission God has given to the church. And it absolutely breaks the back of institutionalism.

4. **Select strategies.** After goals are set, then strategies are the means used to accomplish the goal.[4] A good approach is to consider as many options as possible before selecting a strategy. Several ways may work, but it is wise to use the best way. For example, a church may set a goal to develop an effective evangelism program. There are several options such as small group methods or Sunday school methods. Leaders must wisely decide based on what best fits the church.

Strategies need implementation. This can be as simple as making a decision and starting. Some strategies involve a large number of members, multiple steps, and a budget. Numerous resources are available such as a PERT (Program Evaluation and Review Technique) chart that displays the steps to organize the implementation of a new strategy.[5] Many congregations are also blessed with members who are skilled in all phases of planning. Using their knowledge and skills is good stewardship.

5. *Evaluate progress.* Planning is a process that points the way for the church. It is faith in action, trying to serve God and His purposes. Evaluations inform members of their progress and may identify problems to solve and suggest needed changes.

The evaluation phase of planning is often avoided because it appears judgmental and threatening. Leaders need to reframe the members' understanding of evaluations. In a spiritual context it is a tool for encouraging members and building up the body as they strive to accomplish the mission plans. More often than not, evaluations provide an excellent opportunity to express appreciation to involved Christians and acknowledge their labors of love.

Conclusion

The Center for Church Growth tries to honor God by being a mission-driven ministry. Our mission statement reads:

Equipping churches for growth (Acts 16:5)

To provide a full range of services presenting effective methods that equip churches for spiritual and numerical growth.

Over the past sixteen years the Center has added new services and resources to accomplish our mission. *Measuring Church Growth* was written for the same purpose. It represents helpful insights gained from a large number of churches and hundreds of hours in study and consultation with congregations. My sincere prayer is that it serves as a practical tool to equip church leaders to evaluate and plan effectively. If church leaders will use this resource to plant and water, the evidence is clear. God is still giving the increase.

ENDNOTES

[1] Rick Warren, *The Purpose Driven Church*, p. 111.

[2] C. Kirk Hadaway, *Church Growth Principles*, p. 111.

[3] C. Peter Wagner, *Strategies for Church Growth* (Ventura, CA: Regal, 1987), pp. 170-171.

[4] Ibid., p. 26.

[5] Edward Dayton and Ted Engstrom, *Strategy for Leadership* (Old Tappan, NJ: Revell, 1979), pp. 191-207.

Appendix

Projected DGR Calculations

$\mathbf{A}$ projected DGR calculation is for churches that have less than ten years of data, but would like to have a projected DGR based on their present growth trend. Also, there are times that taking the latest five years of data and projecting a DGR has valuable comparison purposes.

The Church Growth Survey Handbook by Bob Waymire and C. Peter Wagner has become the standard tool for graphing data and calculating growth rates. I highly recommend it as a step-by-step workbook (see the bibliography).

On page 17, they illustrate the calculation procedures. It requires a calculator with y^x and $1/x$ functions. The example on the next page shows each calculator step to determine the DGR for a church of 250 members in 1992, which grew to 425 members by 1997. If you follow the steps with the above figures, your answer should be 189%.

Your Steps	Calculator Display
1. Clear your calculator	0
2. Enter: 425 (latest membership figure)	425
3. Press: ÷	425
4. Enter: 250 (earliest membership)	250
5. Press: =	1.7
6. Press: y^x	1.7
7. Enter: 5 (number of years, 1992-1997)	5
8. Press: 1/x	.2
9. Press: =	1.11
10. Press: y^y	1.11
11. Enter: 10 (ten years)	10
12. Press: = (be sure an answer appears before continuing)	2.89
13. Press: x	2.89
14. Enter: 100	100
15. Press: -	289
16. Enter: 100	100
17. Press: = (this is your DGR)	189%

Selected Bibliography

Barna, George. *Evangelism That Works*. Ventura, CA: Regal, 1995.

Callahan, Kennon L. *Twelve Keys to an Effective Church*. San Francisco: Harper & Row, 1983.

Chaney, Charles L., and Ron S. Lewis. *Design for Church Growth*. Nashville: Broadman, 1977.

Dale, Robert D. *To Dream Again*. Nashville: Broadman, 1981.

Dayton, Edward R., and Ted W. Engstrom. *Strategy for Leadership*. Old Tappan, NJ: Revell, 1979.

Easum, William M. *The Church Growth Handbook*. Nashville: Abingdon, 1990.

Ellas, John W. *Church Growth Through Groups: Strategies for Varying Levels of Christian Community*. Houston, TX: Center for Church Growth, 1990.

_____. *Clear Choices for Churches: Trends Among Growing and Declining Churches of Christ*. Houston, TX: Center for Church Growth, 1994.

George, Carl F. *How to Break Growth Barriers*. Grand Rapids, MI: Baker, 1993.

_____. *Prepare Your Church for the Future*. Tarrytown, NY: Revell, 1991.

George, Carl F., and Robert E. Logan. *Leading and Managing Your Church*. Old Tappan, NJ: Revell, 1987.

Gerber, Vergil. *God's Way to Keep a Church Going and Growing*. Glendale, CA: Regal, 1973.

Gibbs, Eddie. *I Believe in Church Growth*. London: Hodder & Stoughton, 1985.

Hadaway, C. Kirk. *Church Growth Principles: Separating Fact from Fiction*. Nashville: Broadman, 1991.

Hicks, John Mark. "Part One: Numerical Growth in the Theology of Acts." *Church Growth* 11, no. 2 (Second Quarter, 1996): 8-10.

_____. "Part Two: Numerical Growth in the Theology of Acts." *Church Growth* 11, no. 3 (Third Quarter, 1996): 12-13.

Holtz, Darrell. "Numbers: The If and the How." *Christianity Today* 27, no. 10 (June 17, 1983): 65.

Hunter, Kent R. *Foundations for Church Growth*. Corunna, IN: Church Growth Center, 1994.

Jervell, Jacob. *Luke and the People of God*. Minneapolis: Augsburg, 1972.

Lynn, Mac. *Churches of Christ in the United States*. Nashville: Gospel Advocate, 1991.

McGavran, Donald A. *Understanding Church Growth*. 2nd rev. ed. by C. Peter Wagner, Grand Rapids, MI: Eerdmans, 1990.

Miles, Delos. *Church Growth: A Mighty River*. Nashville: Broadman, 1981.

Poloma, Margaret M. and George H. Gallup, Jr. *Varieties of Prayer: A Survey Report*. Philadelphia: Trinity Press International, 1991.

Rainer, Thom S. *The Book of Church Growth: History, Theology, and Principles*. Nashville: Broadman, 1993.

_____. *Effective Evangelistic Churches*. Nashville: Broadman, 1996.

Rothauge, Arlin J. *Sizing Up a Congregation*. New York: Episcopal Church Center.

Schaller, Lyle E. *Looking in the Mirror*. Nashville: Abingdon, 1984.

Smith, Ebbie C. *Balanced Church Growth*. Nashville: Broadman, 1984.

_____. *A Manual for Church Growth Survey*. South Pasadena, CA: William Carey, 1976.

Vaughan, John N. *Megachurches and America's Cities*. Grand Rapids, MI: Baker, 1993.

_____. *The Large Church: a Twentieth Century Expression of the First Century Church*. Grand Rapids, MI: Baker, 1985.

Wagner, C. Peter. *Leading Your Church to Growth*. Ventura, CA: Regal, 1984.

_____. *Strategies for Church Growth*. Ventura, CA: Regal, 1987.

_____. *Your Church Can Be Healthy*. Nashville: Abingdon, 1979.

_____. *Your Church Can Grow*. Ventura, CA: Regal, 1976.

Wagner, C. Peter, and Bob Waymire. *The Church Growth Survey Handbook*. 3rd ed. Colorado Springs: O.C. International, 1994.

Warren, Rick. *The Purpose Driven Church*. Grand Rapids, MI: Zondervan, 1995.

Woods, George O. "What Date Is Worth Your Money." *Pastor's Update Cassettes*. no. 5021, vol. 47, side two.

Yeakley, Flavil R., Jr. *Separating Fact from Fiction: A Realistic Assessment of the Churches of Christ in the United States*. Searcy, AR: Harding Center for Church Growth Studies, 1994.

Index